How to use this book

Matched to the National Curriculum, this Collins Year 1 Targeted Practice Workbook is designed to improve mental maths skills.

Teaching notes to guide you through some of the key aspects of mental maths.

Questions split into three levels of difficulty – **Challenge 1**, **Challenge 2** and **Challenge 3** – to help progression.

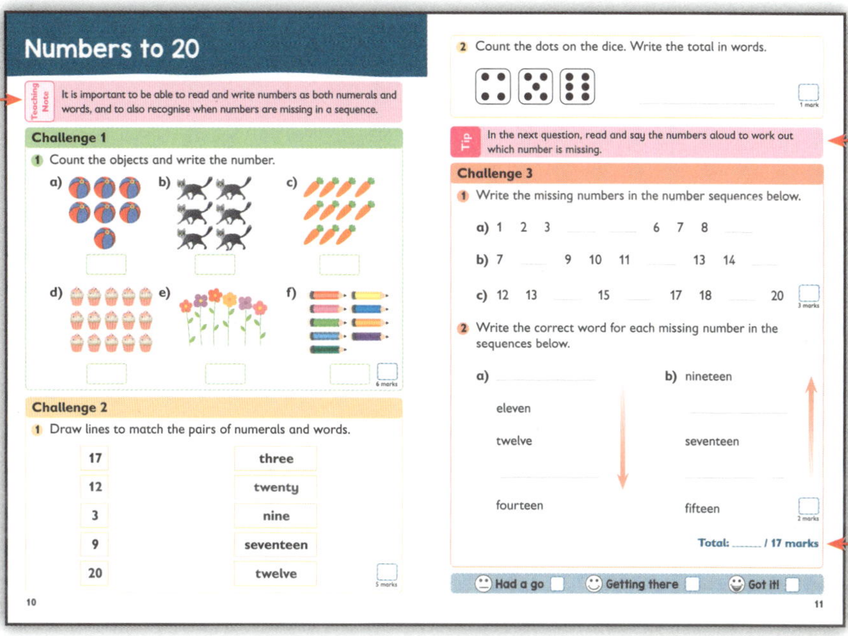

Numbers to 20

Teaching Note: It is important to be able to read and write numbers as both numerals and words, and to also recognise when numbers are missing in a sequence.

Challenge 1

1 Count the objects and write the number.

a) b) c) d) e) f)

6 marks

Challenge 2

1 Draw lines to match the pairs of numerals and words.

17	three
12	twenty
3	nine
9	seventeen
20	twelve

5 marks

10

2 Count the dots on the dice. Write the total in words.

1 mark

Tip: In the next question, read and say the numbers aloud to work out which number is missing.

Challenge 3

1 Write the missing numbers in the number sequences below.

a) 1 2 3 ___ ___ 6 7 8 ___

b) 7 ___ 9 10 11 ___ 13 14 ___

c) 12 13 ___ 15 ___ 17 18 ___ 20

3 marks

2 Write the correct word for each missing number in the sequences below.

a) ___ eleven twelve ___ fourteen

b) nineteen ___ seventeen ___ fifteen

2 marks

Total: ___ / 17 marks

Had a go Getting there Got it!

11

Handy **tips** included throughout.

Total marks boxes for recording progress and **'How am I doing?'** checks for self-evaluation.

Starter test recaps skills covered in Reception class.

Eight **audio tests** that can be accessed using the QR codes provided.

Four **Progress tests** included throughout the book for ongoing assessment and monitoring progress.

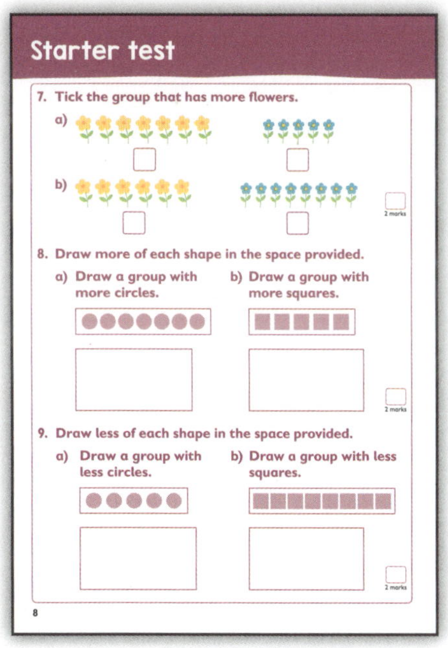

Starter test

7. Tick the group that has more flowers.

a) b)

2 marks

8. Draw more of each shape in the space provided.

a) Draw a group with more circles. b) Draw a group with more squares.

2 marks

9. Draw less of each shape in the space provided.

a) Draw a group with less circles. b) Draw a group with less squares.

2 marks

8

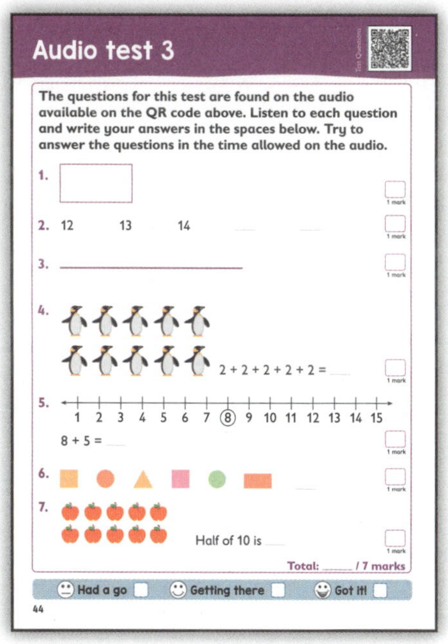

Audio test 3

The questions for this test are found on the audio available on the QR code above. Listen to each question and write your answers in the spaces below. Try to answer the questions in the time allowed on the audio.

1.

2. 12 13 14 ___ ___

3. ___

4. 2 + 2 + 2 + 2 + 2 = ___

5. 1 2 3 4 5 6 7 8 9 10 11 12 13 14 15

8 + 5 = ___

6. ___

7. Half of 10 is ___

Total: ___ / 7 marks

Had a go Getting there Got it!

44

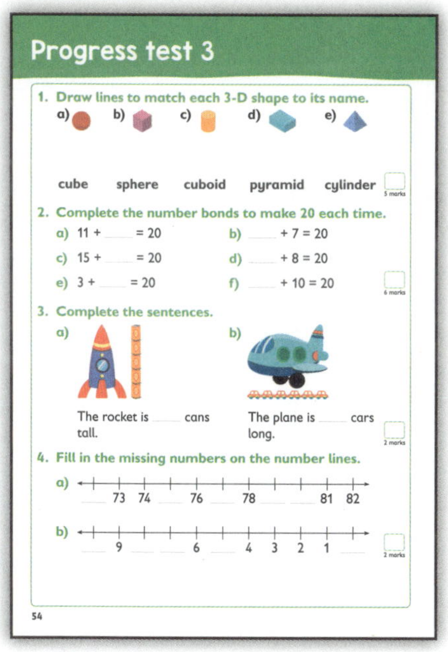

Progress test 3

1. Draw lines to match each 3-D shape to its name.

a) b) c) d) e)

cube sphere cuboid pyramid cylinder

5 marks

2. Complete the number bonds to make 20 each time.

a) 11 + ___ = 20 b) ___ + 7 = 20

c) 15 + ___ = 20 d) ___ + 8 = 20

e) 3 + ___ = 20 f) ___ + 10 = 20

6 marks

3. Complete the sentences.

a) The rocket is ___ cans tall.

b) The plane is ___ cars long.

2 marks

4. Fill in the missing numbers on the number lines.

a) 73 74 76 78 81 82

b) 9 6 4 3 2 1

2 marks

54

Answers are included at the back of the book.

Author: Jon Goulding

Contents

Acknowledgements

The author and publisher are grateful to the copyright holders for permission to use quoted materials and images. All illustrations and images are ©Shutterstock.com and ©HarperCollins*Publishers* Ltd.

Published by Collins
An imprint of HarperCollins*Publishers*
1 London Bridge Street
London SE1 9GF

HarperCollins*Publishers*
Macken House, 39/40 Mayor Street Upper,
Dublin 1, D01 C9W8, Ireland

ISBN 978-0-00-867024-5

First published 2024
This edition published 2025

10 9 8 7 6 5 4 3

British Library Cataloguing in Publication Data.

A CIP record of this book is available from the British Library.

Publisher: Fiona McGlade
Author: Jon Goulding
Commissioning: Richard Toms
Editorial: Fiona Watson
Cover Design: Sarah Duxbury
Inside Concept Design: Ian Wrigley
Typesetting: Contentra Technologies (India)
Production: Bethany Brohm
Printed in the United Kingdom by Martins the Printers

FSC www.fsc.org MIX Paper | Supporting responsible forestry FSC™ C013254

Practising mental maths at home

Why is mental maths practice important?

As young children become increasingly familiar with numbers, shapes and the early stages of developing the four operations of addition, subtraction, multiplication and division, they need to become adept at applying their new skills and understanding mentally. This means being able to instantly recognise numbers, recognise small quantities without counting, and recognise shapes; they should also start making very simple calculations in their head.

Development of strategies and lots of practice ultimately enables methods and models to be committed to longer-term memory, becoming automatic. This in turn frees the shorter-term working memory and enables it to concentrate on more complex calculations. An example of this is being able to instantly know what one or ten more or less than a number is – anything more complex requiring this knowledge can then be tackled more easily because very little thought needs to go into calculating these facts – they are just recalled from memory.

The development of mental maths skills in Year 1 involves more of the 'concrete' learning children have explored in the Early Years Foundation Stage (using real objects to count and manipulate, and handling shapes and money), supported by pictorial representations (the use of pictures of quantities and methods). From time to time, the concrete and the pictorial representations can be withdrawn, with the child working in the abstract, discussing or writing down an aspect of their maths knowledge.

For example, when finding one more than an amount, initially the child may have a number of counters and might count out five of them before placing another counter with the original five and seeing that this makes six (concrete). This can also be represented as pictures or diagrams such as counters on a ten frame or a part-whole model:

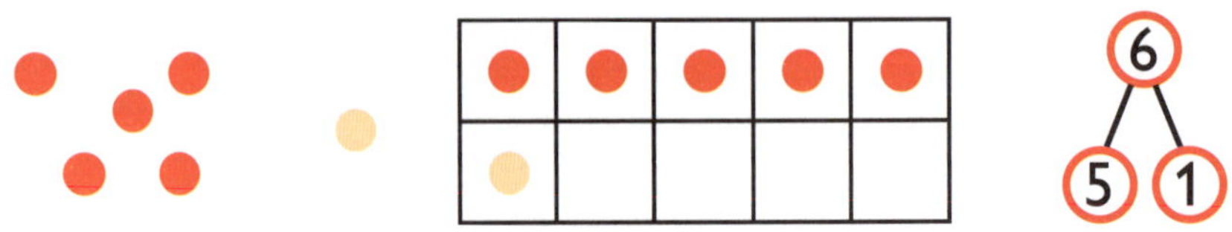

Both pictorial representations show that five and one more is six. Following lots of practice, and discussion, the child may then be able to complete a sentence such as "One more than five is six" or, once introduced to mathematical symbols, be able to complete a calculation such as 5 + 1 = 6 (abstract).

Ultimately, what adults often take for granted as very 'basic' mental calculations also become automatic mental calculations for a child. But beware – the very fact that adults see this as something 'basic' can sometimes lead us to forget that these skills can be tricky to grasp for a child. They need plenty of time, exposure and further support and challenge as they begin to apply their learning.

Mental maths is an incredibly important life skill. As we grow, it is used in everyday tasks such as counting money, measuring lengths and weights and calculating times – for example, how long until the bus comes. Confidence in mental maths and fluency in number facts is key to mathematical problem solving.

In Year 1, children learn the early skills of addition and move on to repeated addition to underpin their understanding of multiplication. All of the maths taught in Year 1 is fundamental in supporting mathematical development in Year 2 and beyond. If these early foundations are not secure enough, learning can become difficult as your child moves on to more complex maths skills.

What you can do at home

Talking about what your child is doing when working through this book and helping them to explain their understanding is highly beneficial – they might want to show you by counting objects, pointing out shapes, turning the hands on a clock face, counting out money or by drawing pictures. This should be encouraged, so you might want to make sure your child has access to pieces of paper, objects for counting, an analogue clock, a range of coins and notes, and a ruler or tape measure.

Additionally, talk about everyday maths such as the time showing on a clock face (o'clock and half past in particular at this stage), about coins you have, or about how you share a pizza or a bar of chocolate, thinking of simple fractions and equal amounts. Ask them about who has the most or least, and about objects that might be taller or shorter, or longer or shorter than others. Continue to develop their language of direction and position, such as left, right, above and below.

You might want to make sure your child has access to:

- objects to count such as counters, cubes or small objects you have many of (and that are all identical)
- paper to make jottings on and to cut shapes from for your child to handle, draw on and fold
- an analogue clock with the numbers 1 to 12 and an hour and minute hand; talk about the difference between the hour and minute hand
- a range of coins and notes to develop a familiarity with money and an understanding of the value of each coin or note
- a ruler or tape measure (with a centimetre scale) to practise early measuring.

Finally, be patient. As already mentioned, these early stages of maths are essential foundations for future learning. And remember, your child should enjoy what they are doing – gentle encouragement and much praise will go a long way to supporting this.

Starter test

1. 1 2 3 4 5 6 7 8 9 10

a) Read the numbers one to ten aloud.

b) Write the numbers one to ten in order in the boxes.

☐ ☐ ☐ ☐ ☐ ☐ ☐ ☐ ☐ ☐

2 marks

2. a) Write the missing numbers on the counters below.

(1) (2) ( ) (4) ( ) (6) ( ) ( ) (9) ( )

b) Some of the counters from one to ten have gone missing. Draw the missing counters below.

3 7 10 4 1

2 marks

3. Write the next three numbers in each sequence.

a) (2) (3) (4) ( ) ( ) ( )

b) (5) (6) (7) ( ) ( ) ( )

2 marks

4. Without counting, write the number of pieces of fruit you see in each picture.

a)  ☐

b)  ☐

c)  ☐

d)  ☐

4 marks

5. **Write the total amount of fruit in each pair of pictures.**

a) 

b) 

c) 

d) 

4 marks

6. **How much pizza will each person have left?**

a) Jaz has three pieces.
She eats one piece.
How many pieces are left?

b) Dylan has four pieces.
He eats one piece.
How many pieces are left?

c) Sal has five pieces.
She eats one piece.
How many pieces are left?

d) Sam has five pieces.
He eats two pieces.
How many pieces are left?

4 marks

7. **Tick the group that has more flowers.**

a)  

☐ ☐

b)  

☐ ☐

2 marks

8. **Draw more of each shape in the space provided.**

a) **Draw a group with more circles.**

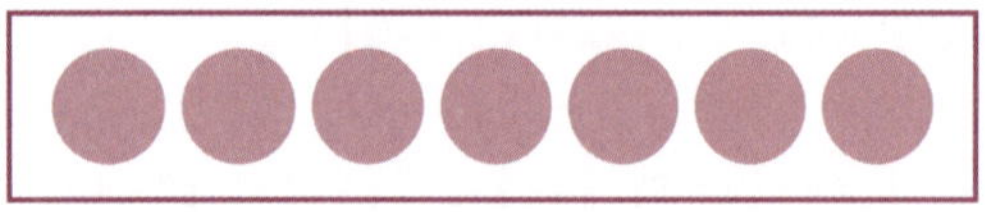

b) **Draw a group with more squares.**

2 marks

9. **Draw less of each shape in the space provided.**

a) **Draw a group with less circles.**

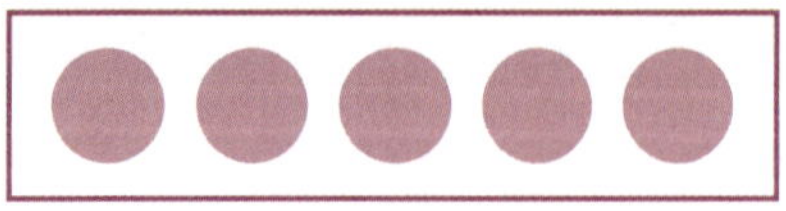

b) **Draw a group with less squares.**

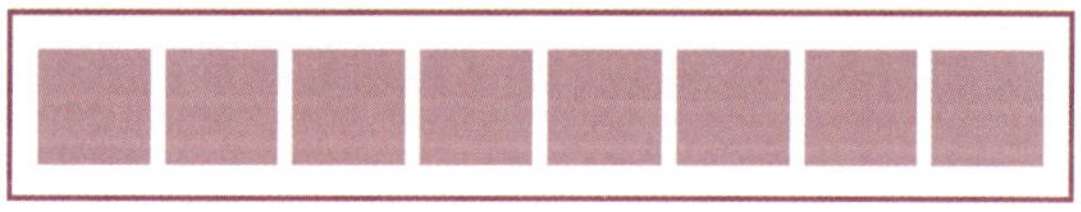

2 marks

10. Draw more shapes to double the number already showing.

a) 

b) 

c) 

d) 

4 marks

11. Write the total number of fish in each pair of pictures.

a) 

b) 

c) 

d) 

4 marks

Total: ______ / 32 marks

Had a go ☐ Getting there ☐ Got it! ☐

Numbers to 20

Teaching Note It is important to be able to read and write numbers as both numerals and words, and to also recognise when numbers are missing in a sequence.

Challenge 1

1 Count the objects and write the number.

a) 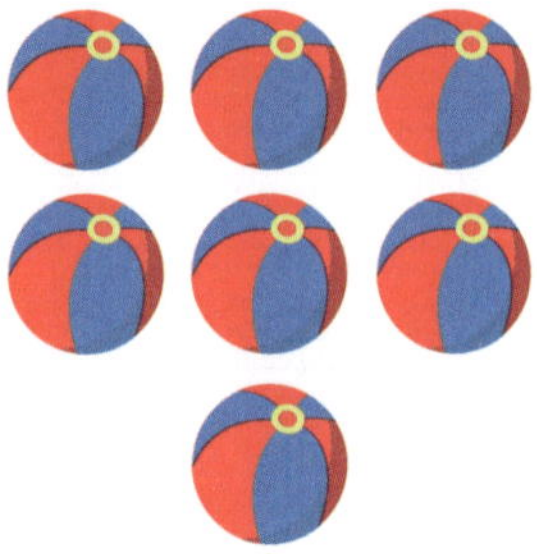

b) 

c) 

d) 

e) 

f) 

6 marks

Challenge 2

1 Draw lines to match the pairs of numerals and words.

17	three
12	twenty
3	nine
9	seventeen
20	twelve

5 marks

2 Count the dots on the dice. Write the total in words.

....

1 mark

Tip In the next question, read and say the numbers aloud to work out which number is missing.

Challenge 3

1 Write the missing numbers in the number sequences below.

a) 1 2 3 .... 6 7 8 ....

b) 7 .... 9 10 11 .... 13 14 ....

c) 12 13 .... 15 .... 17 18 20

3 marks

2 Write the correct word for each missing number in the sequences below.

a) ....

eleven

twelve

....

fourteen

b) nineteen

....

seventeen

....

fifteen

2 marks

Total: ______ / 17 marks

Had a go ☐ **Getting there** ☐ **Got it!** ☐

One more and one less

Teaching Note Recognising the number **one more** and **one less** than a given number consolidates sequencing skills and forms the basis of addition and subtraction.

Challenge 1

1 Draw one more of each shape and write the new number of shapes shown.

a)  ....

b) 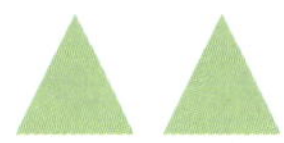 ....

c)  ....

d)  ....

4 marks

Tip In the next question, count the number of objects, then cover up one object (or cross it out) and count them again to find one less.

Challenge 2

1 Write the number that is one less than the number of objects shown.

a)  ....

b)  ....

c)  ....

d)  ....

4 marks

Tip

Looking at numbers on a number line is useful when beginning to identify which number is one more or one less than a given number.

1 2 3 4 5 6 7 8 9 10 11 12 13 14 15 16 17 18 19 20

Challenge 3

1 Complete each statement with the correct number.

a) 1 more than 7 is ....

b) 1 more than 17 is ....

c) 1 less than 4 is ....

d) 1 less than 14 is ....

e) 1 less than 9 is ....

f) 1 more than 9 is ....

g) 1 less than 10 is ....

h) 1 less than 20 is ....

8 marks

2 Use the words **more** or **less** to complete each statement.

a) 17 is one .... than 16

b) 2 is one .... than 3

c) 16 is one .... than 17

d) 10 is one .... than 11

e) 19 is one .... than 18

f) 13 is one .... than 14

6 marks

Total: ______ / 22 marks

Had a go ☐ Getting there ☐ Got it! ☐

Comparing amounts and numbers

Teaching Note Understanding the concepts of more than, less than, most and least, two equal amounts and the phrase **equal to** is a crucial step in beginning to consider calculations in maths.

Challenge 1

1. Under each set of objects write the words **most** and **least** to correspond with the number of objects.

   a) 

   ....

   b) 

   ....

2 marks

Challenge 2

1. Draw the number of shapes **equal to** the number shown in each picture.

   a) is equal to

   b) is equal to

2 marks

2. In each pair, draw additional shapes in the second picture to make it **equal to** the first picture.

   a)

b)

2 marks

Challenge 3

1 Write the words **equal to**, **more than** or **less than** in the spaces provided.

a) 

is .... six

b) 

is .... seven

c) 19 is 18

d) 16 is 16

e) 10 is 8

f) 13 is 17

6 marks

2 Use the numbers from the counters below to make each statement correct.

5 5 7 10 11 12 13 16 18 20

a) .... is equal to ....

b) .... is less than ....

c) .... is less than ....

d) .... is less than ....

e) .... is less than ....

f) .... is more than ....

6 marks

Total: ______ / 18 marks

Had a go ☐ Getting there ☐ Got it! ☐

Number bonds

Teaching Note Children need to have an understanding that numbers can be split into different **parts**. For example, the **whole** number six can be made up of three and three, or two and four, or two and two and two, etc.

Challenge 1

1 Complete each pair of part-whole models by counting the number of dots. One has been done for you.

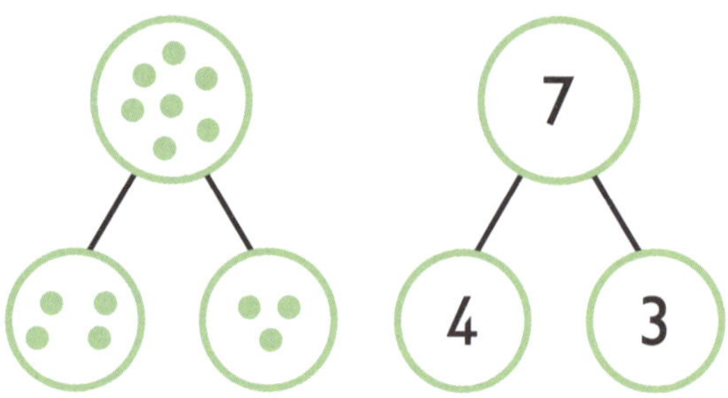

a) 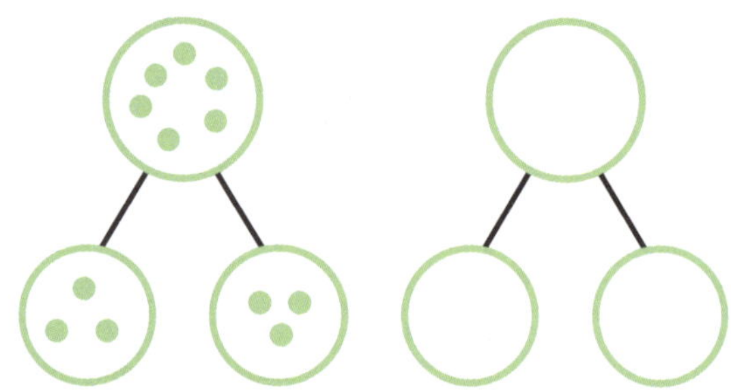

b) 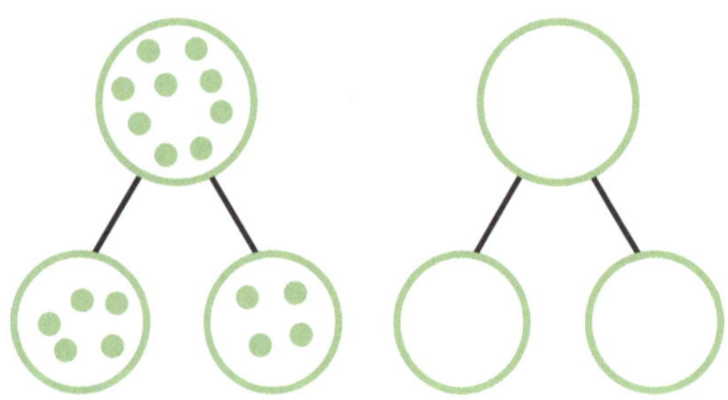

c) 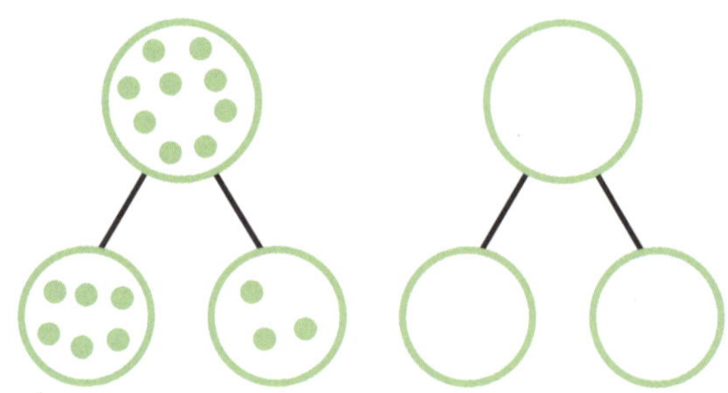

3 marks

2 Complete the part-whole models and the sentences. The whole number has been given to help you think of the parts.

a) 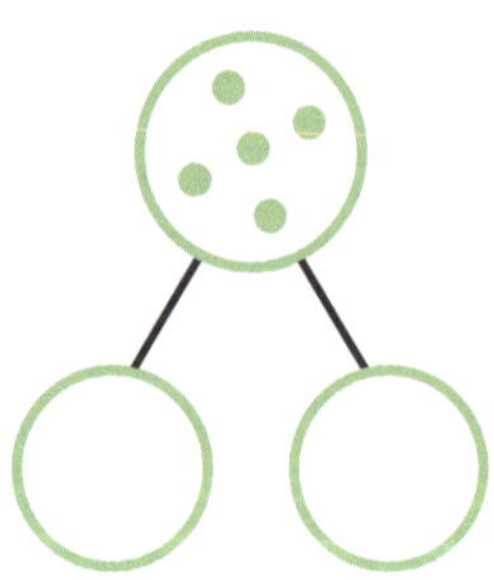

b) 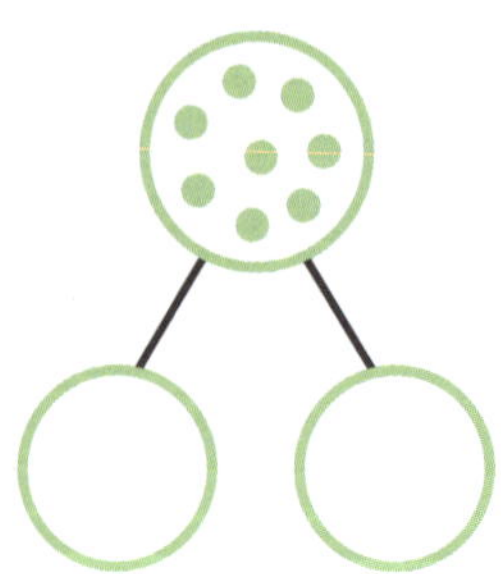

c) 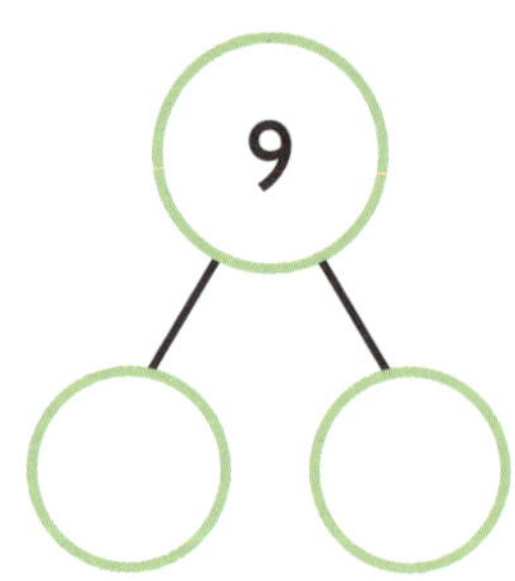

a) .... is the whole.
The parts are .... and ....

b) .... is the whole.
The parts are .... and ....

c) .... is the whole.
The parts are .... and ....

3 marks

Teaching Note Explain that when parts are put together to make a whole it is called addition and uses the + symbol. An example sentence is three plus two equals five, or 3 + 2 = 5.

Challenge 2

1 The red and yellow counters in each tens frame are the two parts. Write the number sentence that is represented in each frame. The first one has been started for you.

a) 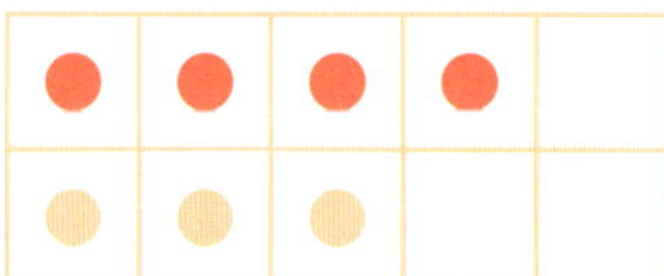

4 + 3 = ...

b) 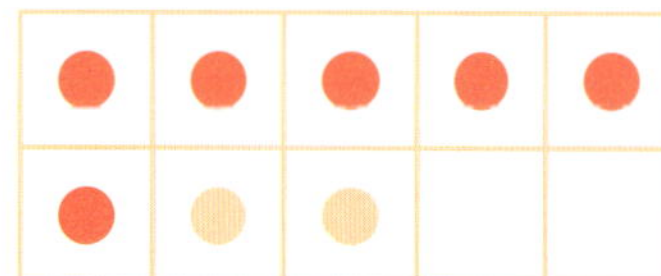

.... + ... = ...

2 marks

2 The whole number for each of these tens frames should be 10. Only the red counters have been drawn. Draw the other counters and complete the number sentences.

a) 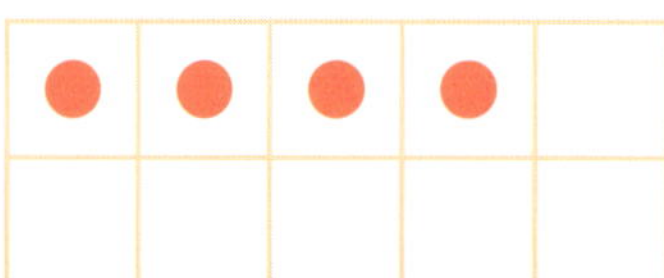

.... + ... = ...

b) 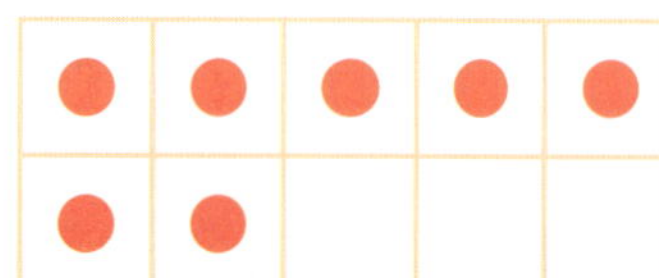

.... + ... = ...

2 marks

Challenge 3

1 Complete the number bond families represented by the part-whole models. The first one has been started for you.

a) 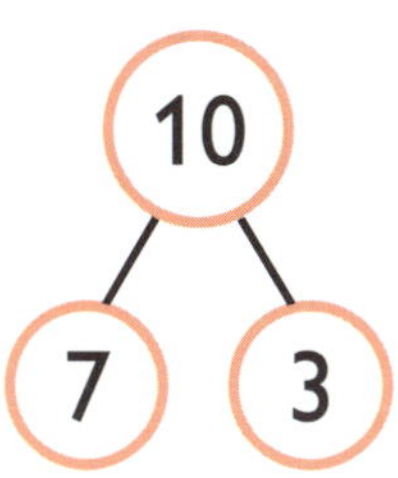

7 + 3 = ...

.... + 7 = 10

b) 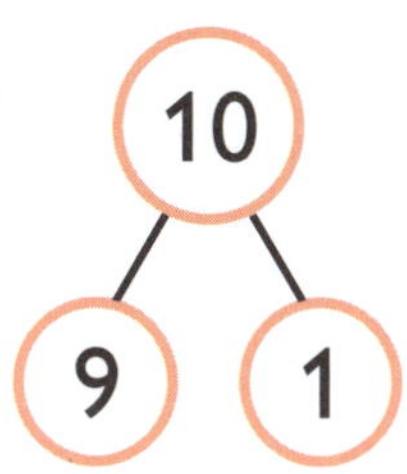

.... + ... = ...

.... + ... = ...

2 marks

Total: ______ / 12 marks

Had a go ☐ Getting there ☐ Got it! ☐

Length and height

Teaching Note Ensure that the words **long** and **short** and **tall** and **short** are used correctly when referring to **length** and **height**. These words become **longer**, **shorter** and **taller** when making comparisons.

Challenge 1

1 Write the word **longer** or **shorter** in the space provided for each pair of lines, then say the word.

a) The blue line is ....

b) The red line is ....

c) The green line is ....

d) The pink line is ....

4 marks

2 Write the word **taller** or **shorter** in the space provided for each picture, then say the word.

a) This tree is .... than Amy.

b) Dan is .... than this tree.

2 marks

Challenge 2

1 Draw taller or shorter stick people as instructed.

a) Draw a taller person than the one shown.

b) Draw a shorter person than the one shown.

2 marks

Teaching Note Measuring of length and height begins with non-standard units such as counting cubes or boxes before moving on to centimetres. At this stage, it becomes important to look at a ruler and to discuss how it works.

Challenge 3

1 Complete the sentences.

a) Troy is the same height as six boxes.

Troy is .... boxes tall.

b) Zara's mouse is as long as one pencil.

Zara's pet mouse is .... pencil long.

2 marks

2 Use the ruler pictures to work out the lengths and heights of the objects.

a) The doll is .... cm tall.

b) The pencil is .... cm long.

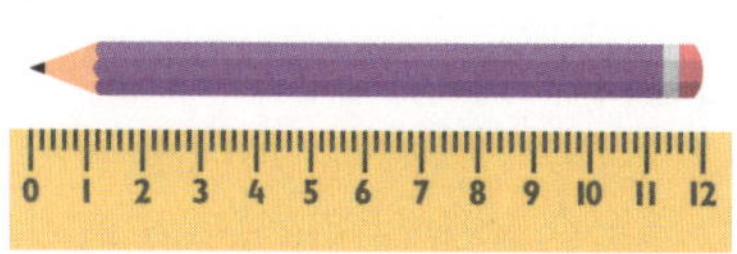

c) The length of the toy train is .... cm

d) The height of the mug is .... cm

4 marks

Total: ______ / 14 marks

Had a go ☐ Getting there ☐ Got it! ☐

Days, weeks and months

Challenge 1

1 Write the names of the days of the week in the correct order. The first one has been done for you.

Tuesday Saturday Monday Friday Thursday Sunday Wednesday

Monday ....

....

6 marks

2 Complete the statements below with the words **before** or **after**.

a) Monday is .... Wednesday.

b) Saturday is .... Thursday.

c) June is .... April.

d) October is .... November.

4 marks

3 There are 12 months in a year. Write the names of the missing months in the correct order.

.... February March ....

May .... July ....

September .... December

6 marks

4 Complete the facts about months.

a) The first month of the year is ....

b) The last month of the year is ....

c) The month before April is ....

3 marks

Challenge 2

1 There are seven days in one week. Write the correct answers about the weeks.

a) How many days are there in two weeks?

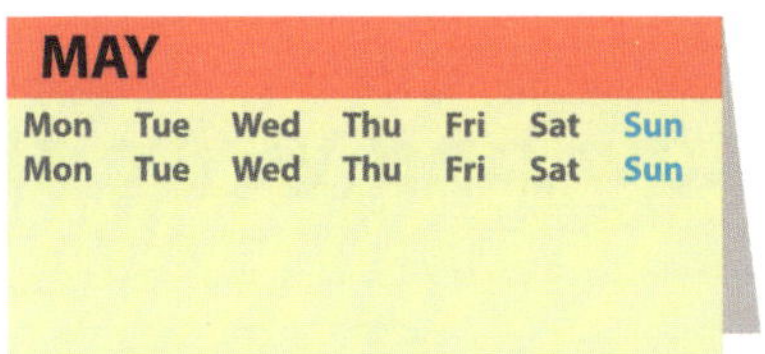

There are .... days in two weeks.

b) How many days are there in three weeks?

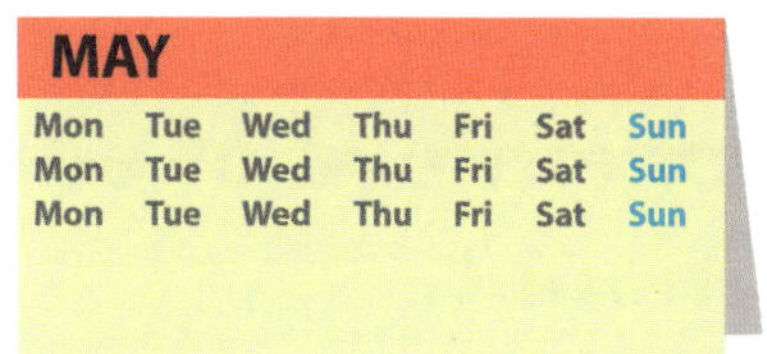

There are .... days in three weeks.

2 marks

Challenge 3

1 Use the calendars to help you answer the questions.

a) How many weeks are there in February? .... weeks

b) How many weeks are printed in red on the calendar? .... weeks

c) Highlight two weeks on this calendar.

3 marks

Total: ______ / 24 marks

Had a go ☐ Getting there ☐ Got it! ☐

Progress test 1

1. Write the names and numerals for the missing numbers.

a) .... six seven .... nine ten .... twelve

.... 6 7 .... 9 10 12

b) .... fourteen .... sixteen

.... 14 16

2 marks

2. Draw one more of each shape below and write the new amount.

a)  ....

b)  ....

c)  ....

d)  ....

4 marks

3. Write the number one less than the number of each animal shown.

a) 

b) 

c) 

3 marks

4. **Use the ruler pictures to work out the length or height of these objects.**

a) The flower is .... cm tall.

b) The grasshopper is .... cm long.

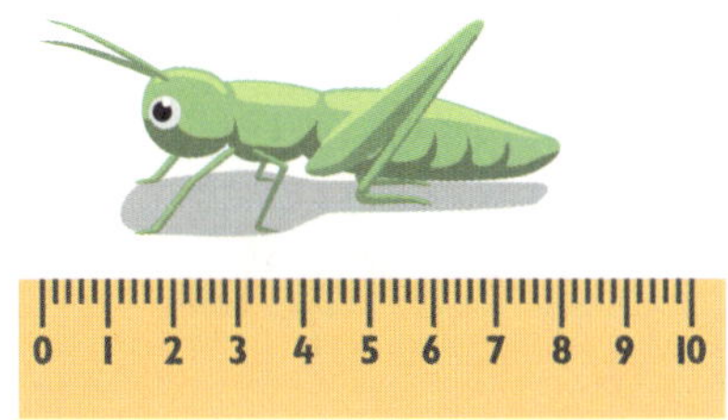

2 marks

5. **Carlo gets a badge for each month he runs in the park race.**

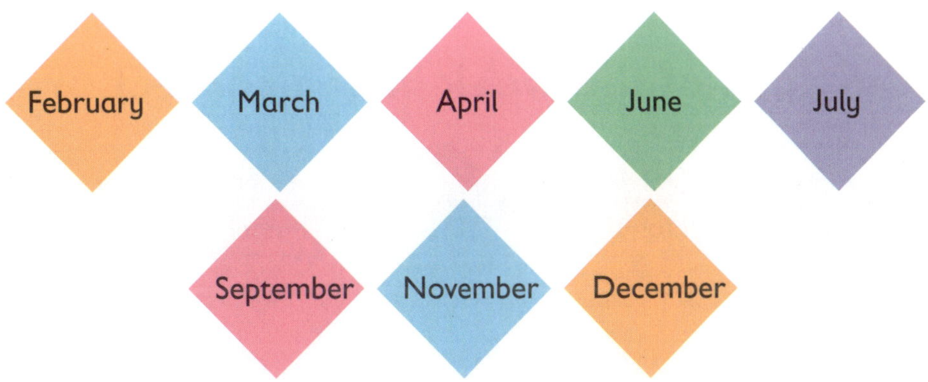

Which months did Carlo miss the park race?

....

1 mark

6. **Draw lines that are longer and shorter than the one shown.**

2 marks

7. **Complete the number bond pairs represented by each tens frame.**

a) 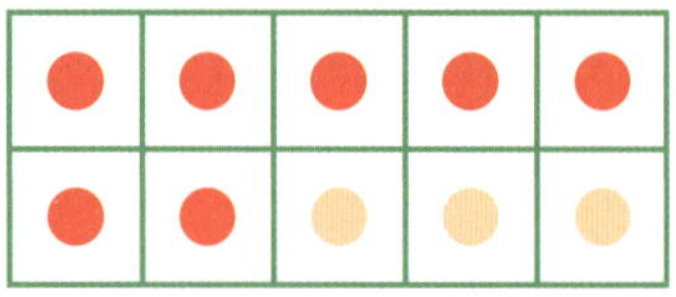

...... + ... = ...

...... + ... = ...

b) 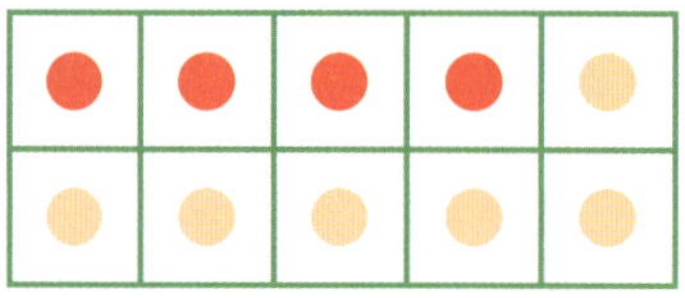

...... + ... = ...

...... + ... = ...

c) 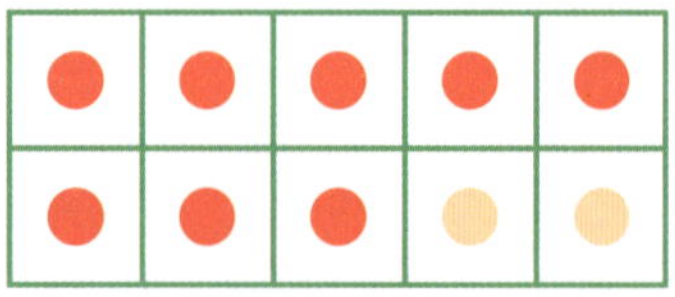

...... + ... = ...

...... + ... = ...

3 marks

8. **Write the days of the week in the correct order.**

......

......

1 mark

9. **Write the words equal to, more than or less than to make these statements true.**

a)  is ...... eight

b) 12 is 13

c) 20 is 10

3 marks

10. Zara thinks of a number. It is more than 12 and it is less than 17. It is an even number.

a) What two numbers could Zara be thinking of? ....

b) She then says her number is one more than 15

What is her number? ....

2 marks

11. Kevin has drawn a part-whole model to represent 5 + 3 = 8

Explain what Kevin has done wrong.

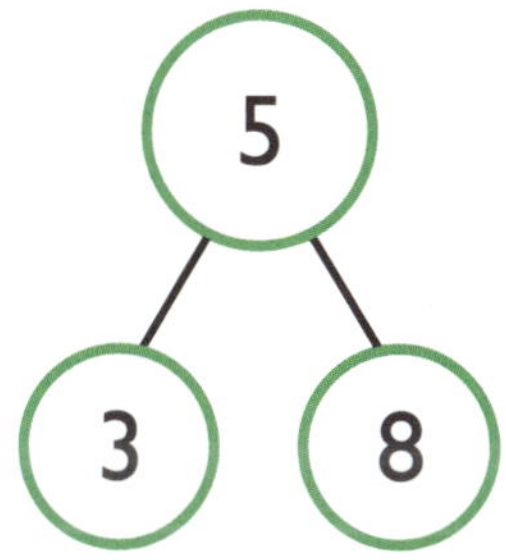

....

....

1 mark

Tip Throughout this book, your child could give answers that involve providing an explanation verbally rather than writing them.

12. Priti grows two flowers. One is taller than her, the other is shorter.

a) Draw a flower taller than Priti.

b) Draw a flower shorter than Priti.

2 marks

taller shorter

Total: ______ / 26 marks

Had a go ☐ Getting there ☐ Got it! ☐

Audio test 1

Test Questions

The questions for this test are found on the audio available on the QR code above. Listen to each question and write your answers in the spaces below. Try to answer the questions in the time allowed on the audio.

1. .... 1 mark

2. ________________________ ☐

________________________________ ☐ 1 mark

3. .... 1 mark

4. .... 1 mark

5.  .... 1 mark

6. 3 7 10 11 16 17 1 mark

7. .... 1 mark

8. 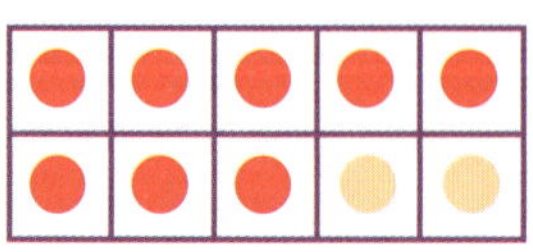 .... + ... = 10 1 mark

Total: ______ / 8 marks

Had a go ☐ Getting there ☐ Got it! ☐

Audio test 2

Test Questions

The questions for this test are found on the audio available on the QR code above. Listen to each question and write your answers in the spaces below. Try to answer the questions in the time allowed on the audio.

1. 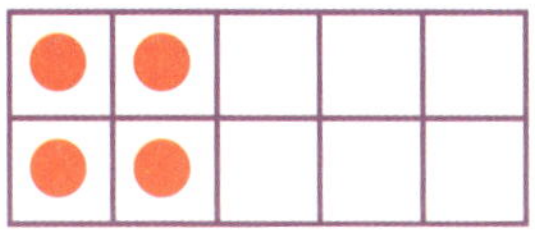

1 mark

2.  ....

1 mark

3. Tuesday, Wednesday, Thursday, Friday, Saturday, Sunday

....

1 mark

4. 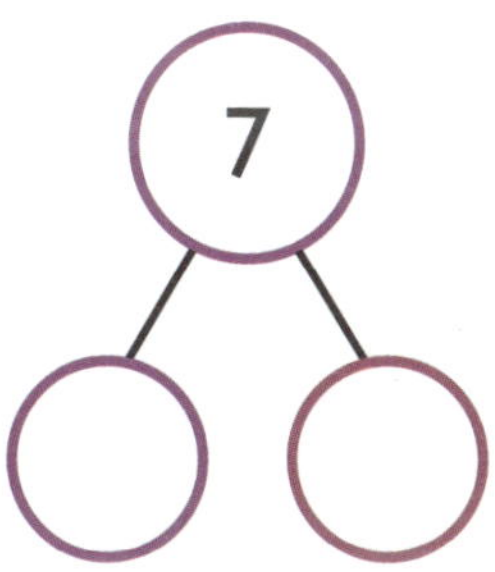

1 mark

5. 

1 mark

6. ....

1 mark

7. five six seven eight nine ten eleven twelve

1 mark

8. .... + ... = ...

1 mark

Total: ______ / 8 marks

Had a go ☐ Getting there ☐ Got it! ☐

Numbers to 100 and beyond

Teaching Note When using 100 squares, ensure that there is an understanding of the need to return to the beginning of the next row when counting forwards. Listen to the numbers being read aloud.

Challenge 1

1 Read each number on the 100 square aloud. Write the missing numbers in the empty squares.

1	2	3	4	5	6	7	8		10
11		13	14	15		17	18	19	20
21	22		24	25	26	27	28	29	30
31		33	34	35	36	37	38	39	40
41	42	43	44		46	47	48	49	50
51	52	53		55	56	57	58	59	60
	62	63	64	65	66	67	68	69	
71	72	73	74	75	76	77		79	80
81	82	83	84	85	86		88		90
91	92			95	96	97	98	99	

15 marks

Challenge 2

1 Count forwards and fill in the missing numbers.

a) 32 .... 35 .... 37 38 .... 40 ....

b) 67 .... 69 .... 71 .... 74 76

2 marks

2 Count backwards and fill in the missing numbers.

a) 53 .... 50 .... 48 47 44

b) .... 99 98 .... 95 .... 93 92 ....

2 marks

Challenge 3

1 Fill in the missing numbers on these sections of 100 squares.

a)

44		46	
54			57
	65		67
	75	76	

b)

67			70
	88	89	90
97		99	100

2 marks

2 Fill in the missing numbers in the sequences.

a) 97 .... 99 .... 102 .... 104 105 107

b) (105) (104) ( ) (102) ( ) ( ) ( )

2 marks

3 Complete the number line by counting forwards from 136

[ ] [ ] [ ] [ ] [ ] [ ]

1 mark

4 Complete the number line by counting backwards from 202

[ ] [ ] [ ] [ ] [ ] [ ]

1 mark

Total: ______ / 25 marks

Had a go ☐ Getting there ☐ Got it! ☐

Addition and subtraction 1

Teaching Note Recap the addition symbol + and explain that this shows that two amounts will be added together to find a new total. Explain that the minus symbol – is used to show that an amount will be taken away (subtracted) from an amount to find a new total.

Challenge 1

1 Count the total number of objects to find each total. Complete the part-whole model then say the number sentence out loud.

a)  + = ...

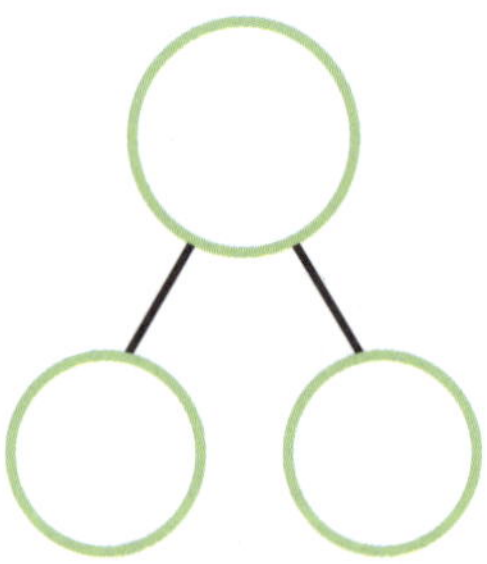

b)  + = ...

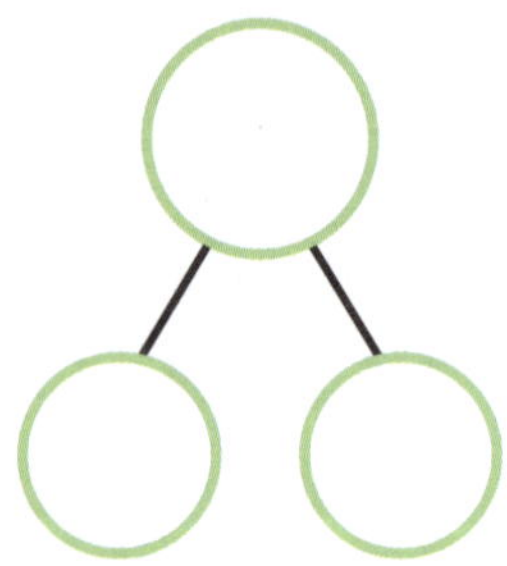

2 marks

Challenge 2

1 Cross out one object from each picture to find the new total and write it in the number sentence. Use the part-whole models to help you. Say each number sentence out loud.

a) 

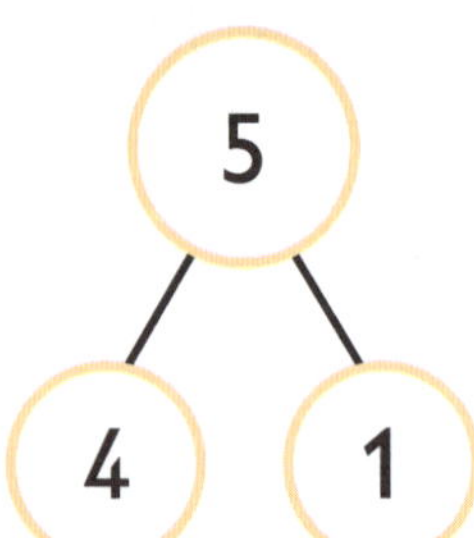

5 – 1 = ...

b) 

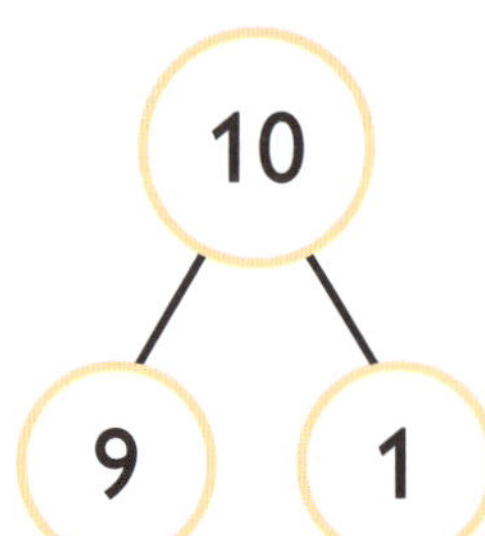

10 – 1 = ...

2 marks

Teaching Note

Number lines can be used to help with counting on and counting back to find more or less than a number. 'Jumps', as shown in the example below, can be used to see the **addition** or **subtraction**.

Challenge 3

1 Use the number lines to find the amount **more** than the circled starting number. One has been done for you.

3 more than 7 is 10 $7 + 3 = 10$

a)

4 more than 5 is .... + ... = ...

b)

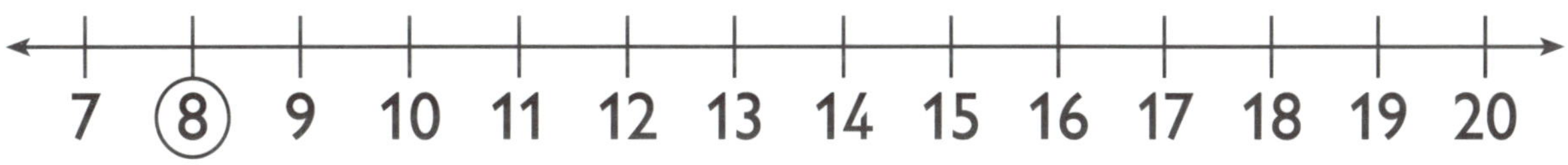

7 more than 8 is .... + ... = ...

2 marks

2 Use the number lines to find the amount **less** than the circled starting number. One has been done for you.

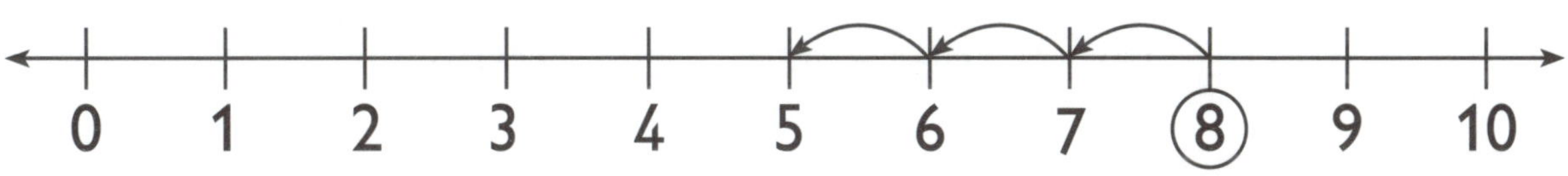

3 less than 8 is 5 $8 - 3 = 5$

a)

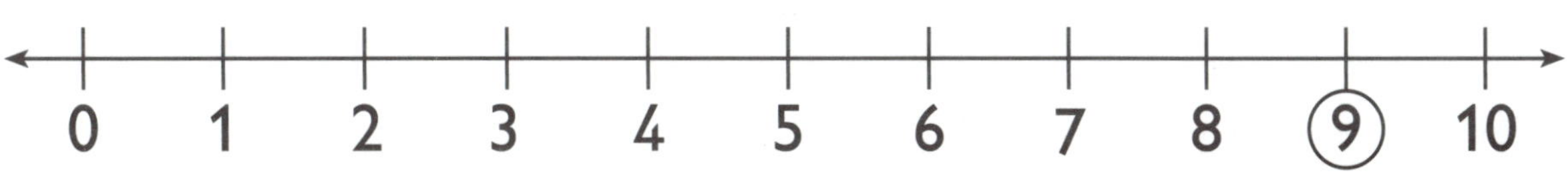

9 less than 9 is .... – .... = ...

b)

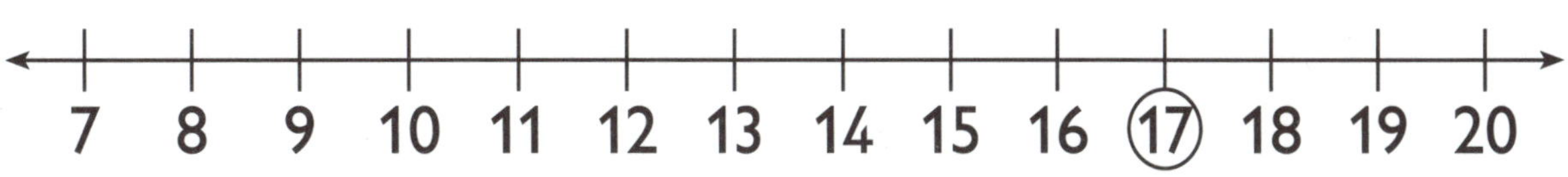

5 less than 17 is .... – .... = ...

2 marks

Total: ______ / 8 marks

Had a go ☐ Getting there ☐ Got it! ☐

Multiplication

Teaching Note The first stages in learning multiplication consider repeated addition as a representation of several equal groups.

Challenge 1

1 Count the objects and fill in the answers.

a) 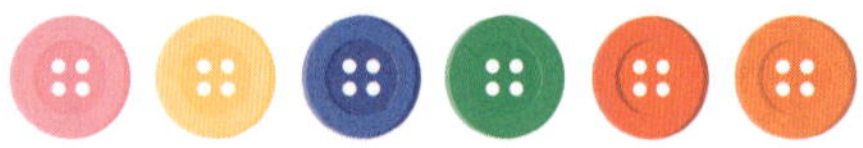 1 + 1 + 1 + 1 + 1 + 1 = ...

There are .... buttons.

b)  2 + 2 + 2 + 2 = ...

There are .... socks.

2 marks

Tip Repeated addition can be represented by an array – an arrangement of objects into columns and rows.

Challenge 2

1 Complete the repeated addition for each array.

a) In the array below there are .... groups of two.

.... + ... + ... + ... + ... = ...

b) In the array below there are .... groups of five.

.... + ... + ... + ... = ...

2 marks

Teaching Note To represent repeated addition as multiplication, the × symbol is used.

Challenge 3

1 Complete the repeated addition and multiplication for each array.

a) 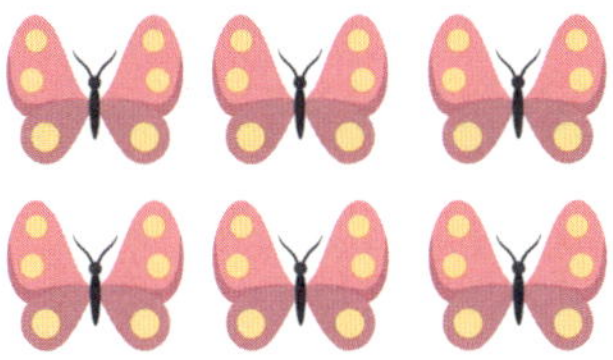

2 + 2 + 2 = 6 or

3 × 2 = ☐ or 2 × 3 = ☐

b) 

3 + 3 + 3 + 3 = ☐ or

4 × 3 = ☐ or 3 × 4 = ☐

☐ 2 marks

2 Draw an array and write the answer for each repeated addition and multiplication.

a) 2 + 2 + 2 + 2 + 2 + 2 + 2 = ... 7 × 2 = ...

b) 3 + 3 + 3 = ... 3 × 3 = ...

☐ 2 marks

Total: ______ / 8 marks

Had a go ☐ Getting there ☐ Got it! ☐

Comparing time

Challenge 1

1 Use the words **before** or **after** to complete these sentences.

a) Rav rides his bike .... playing in the park.

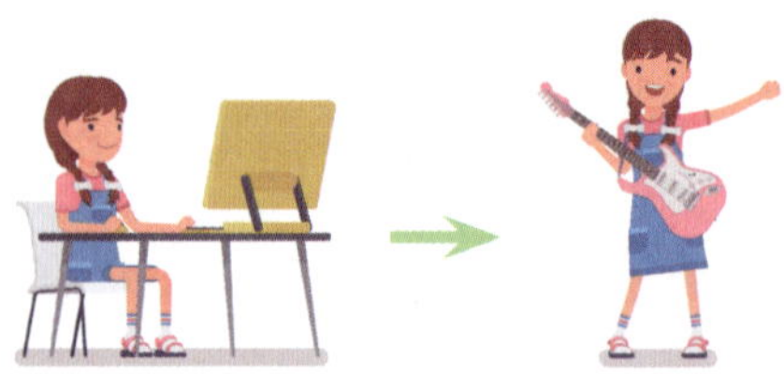

b) Alex plays her guitar .... school.

2 marks

2 Use the words **later** or **earlier** to complete the sentences.

a)

Olly goes to bed .... than his sister.

b)

The cat is awake .... than the dog.

2 marks

3 Add a number to each sentence to make a statement that is correct.

a) .... o'clock is later than one o'clock.

b) .... o'clock is earlier than 11 o'clock.

2 marks

Challenge 2

1 Look at the times on the clocks below.

a) Tick **true** or **false** for each statement in the table below.

	True	False
8 o'clock is later than 9 o'clock.		
Piotr eats his lunch later than brushing his teeth.		
School starts earlier than 12 o'clock.		

b) The earliest time shown on the clocks is ....

c) The latest time shown on the clocks is ....

5 marks

Challenge 3

1 Look at the pictures showing how long it took each child to finish the sponsored walk.

a) Tick **true** or **false** for each statement in the table below.

	True	False
Only Neesa finished in less than two hours.		
Molly was ten seconds quicker than Cam.		
Cam was four seconds quicker than Neesa.		

b) The person finishing first was ....

c) The person finishing second was ....

5 marks

Total: ______ / 16 marks

Had a go ☐ Getting there ☐ Got it! ☐

Half

Teaching Note

Understanding half as one of two equal parts of a whole shape or quantity is a skill that underpins work with fractions in later year groups. Ensure that there is an understanding that two halves of an object are equal, and that whole represents both halves (the whole shape or whole amount).

Challenge 1

1 Shade half of each shape. One has been done for you.

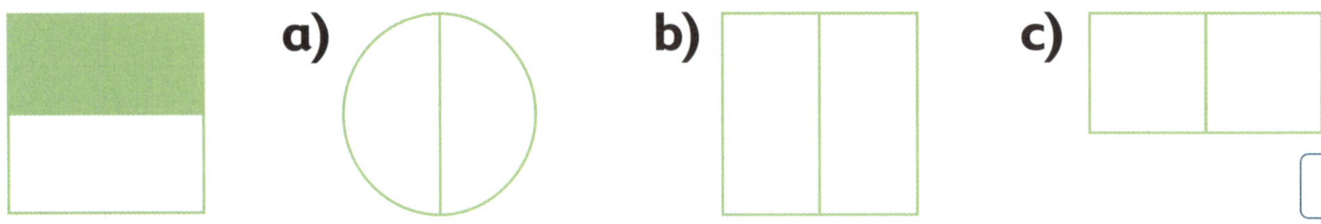

3 marks

2 Tick (✓) each shape that has a half shaded.
One has been done for you.

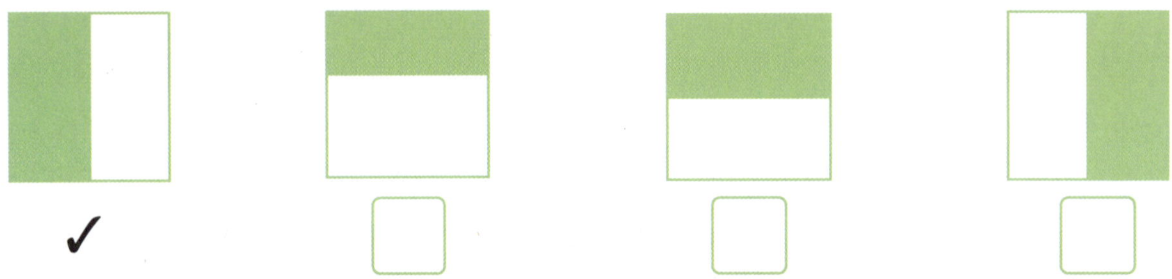

2 marks

Challenge 2

1 Draw a straight line to divide each shape into two halves.

4 marks

2 Half can be written as $\frac{1}{2}$. Write $\frac{1}{2}$ under each half pizza.

2 marks

Teaching Note Finding half of a quantity requires further understanding that both halves are an equal amount.

Challenge 3

1 Draw a line to spilt each set of objects into equal parts. Complete the sentence to show half of the amount. One has been done for you.

a) 

b) 

Half of 6 = 3

Half of 8 = ☐

Half of 4 = ☐

2 marks

2 Only half of each set of shapes has been drawn. Complete each set of shapes by drawing the other half and completing the sentence with the full amount.

a) 

5 is half of ....

b) 

6 is half of ....

c) 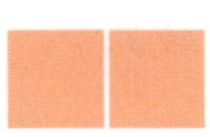

2 is half of ....

d) 

8 is half of ....

4 marks

Total: ______ / 17 marks

Had a go ☐ Getting there ☐ Got it! ☐

2-D and 3-D shapes

Teaching Note

The names of 2-D and 3-D shapes should be discussed and, where possible, real examples of the shapes should be found to enable a greater appreciation through handling each shape.

Challenge 1

1 Draw lines to match each of the shapes below to its name.

a)  **circle** **b)**  **triangle**

c)  **square** **d)**  **rectangle**

4 marks

2 Complete the sentences about 2-D shapes.

a) A square has .... sides.

b) A triangle has .... corners.

c) A rectangle has .... corners.

d) A shape with three sides is a ....

4 marks

Challenge 2

1 Write the name of each shape from the choices below.

cube **sphere** **cuboid** **pyramid** **cylinder**

a) A dice is the shape of a ....

b) In Egypt you can see a giant ....

c) A ball is a ....

d) This box is a ....

e) This beaker is a ....

5 marks

Challenge 3

1 Recognising 2-D and 3-D shapes.

a) Draw a circle around each of the triangles.

b) Draw a circle around each square.

c) Draw a circle around each cuboid.

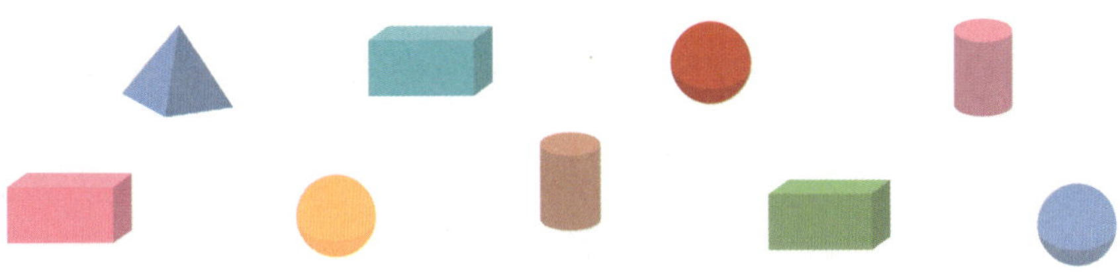

3 marks

2 Sorting 2-D and 3-D shapes.

a) Draw a circle around the 2-D shapes.

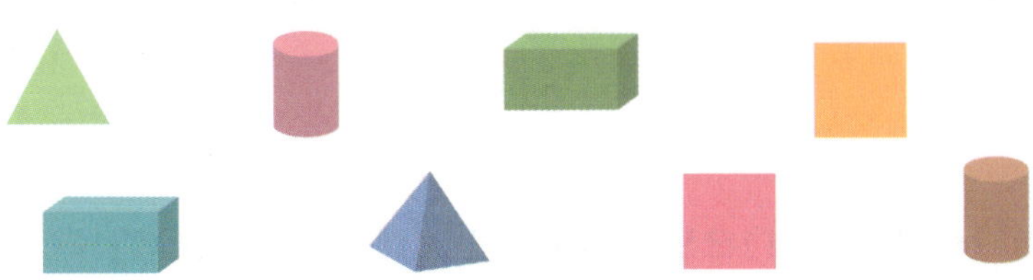

b) Draw a circle around the 3-D shapes.

2 marks

Total: ______ / 18 marks

Had a go ☐ Getting there ☐ Got it! ☐

Progress test 2

1. Look at the stick people below.

Grace Kat

a) Kat says her stick person is 10 cm tall. Explain whether she is right or wrong.

....

b) Grace's stick person is taller.

True ☐ False ☐

2 marks

2. Fill in the missing numbers on these sections of 100 squares.

a)

11		13	
	22		24
31	32		
		43	44

b)

56			59
	67	68	
		78	79
86			

2 marks

3. These five clocks show times in the afternoon and evening. Order them by writing the numbers 1 to 5 to show the times from earliest to latest.

☐ ☐ ☐ ☐ ☐

1 mark

4. Complete the repeated addition for each array below.

a) In the array below there are .... groups of three.

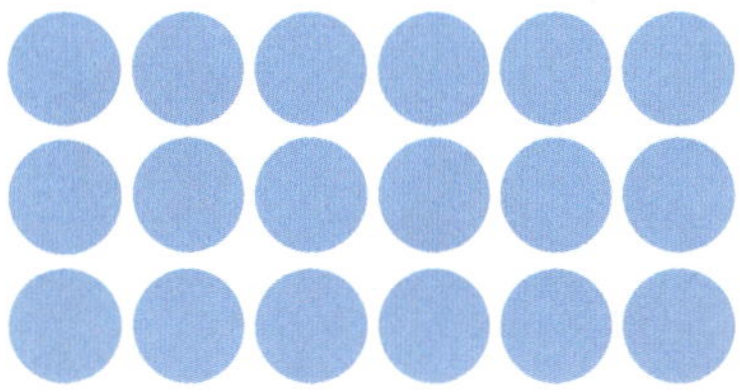

.... + ... + ... + ... + ... + ... = ...

b) In the array below there are .... groups of four.

.... + ... + ... + ... = ...

2 marks

5. Circle the shapes that have half shaded.

a)  **b)**  **c)**  **d)** 

2 marks

6. Write the numbers that are one less and one more than the number of objects shown.

a)  one more is .... one less is ....

b)  one more is .... one less is ....

2 marks

Progress test 2

7. Look at the shapes.

a) How many triangles are there? ....

b) How many circles are there? ....

c) How many squares are there? ....

3 marks

8. There are eight halves of pizza. How many whole pizzas does this make?

Eight half pizzas is the same as .... whole pizzas.

1 mark

9. Ella is thinking of 2-D shapes. She gives a clue for each one. Write the name of each shape she is thinking of. Use the words below to help you.

square **triangle** **circle**

a) It has three sides. ....

b) It has four sides all the same length. ....

c) It has no corners. ....

3 marks

10. Ravi says half of the sweets he has is four.

Draw the sweets in two groups to show why he is incorrect.

1 mark

11. Complete the number bonds to make ten each time.

a) 1 + ... = 10   b) 7 + ... = 10   c) 4 + ... = 10

d) .... + 8 = 10   e) .... + 5 = 10   f) .... + 0 = 10

6 marks

12. The classroom calendar shows the school holiday dates in green.

a) How many weeks is the school holiday? .... weeks

b) How many days is this?

.... days

c) Jaz will spend one week of the holiday at her nan's house. How many days will this be?

.... days

3 marks

Total: ________ / 28 marks

Had a go ☐   Getting there ☐   Got it! ☐

Audio test 3

Test Questions

The questions for this test are found on the audio available on the QR code above. Listen to each question and write your answers in the spaces below. Try to answer the questions in the time allowed on the audio.

1.

1 mark

2. 12 13 14 ....

1 mark

3. ______________________________

1 mark

4.

2 + 2 + 2 + 2 + 2 = ...

1 mark

5. 1 2 3 4 5 6 7 (8) 9 10 11 12 13 14 15

8 + 5 = ...

1 mark

6.

....

1 mark

7.

Half of 10 is ....

1 mark

Total: ______ / 7 marks

Had a go ☐ Getting there ☐ Got it! ☐

Audio test 4

Test Questions

The questions for this test are found on the audio available on the QR code above. Listen to each question and write your answers in the spaces below. Try to answer the questions in the time allowed on the audio.

1.

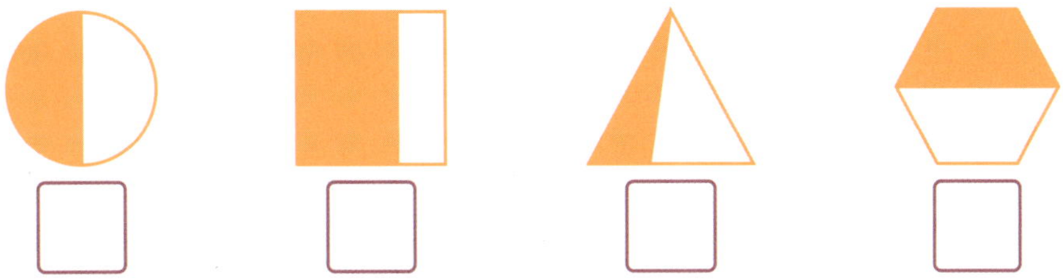

1 mark

2.

9 – 1 = ...

1 mark

3.

33 .... 29 .... 26 25 24

1 mark

4.

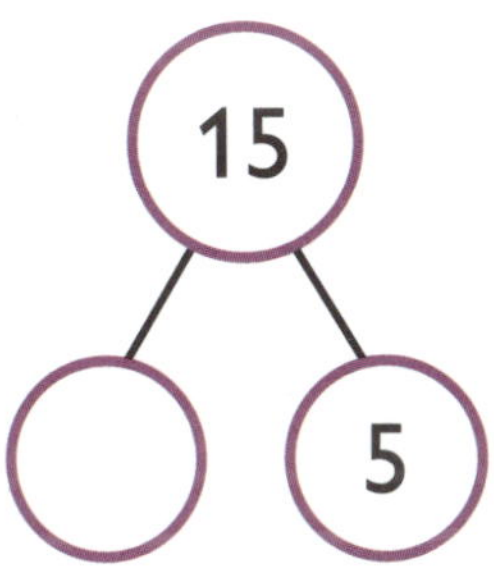

1 mark

5.

....

1 mark

6.

a) The earliest time is ....

b) The latest time is ....

2 marks

Total: ______ / 7 marks

Had a go ☐ Getting there ☐ Got it! ☐

Addition and subtraction 2

Challenge 1

1 Count the fruit to help find the total of the two numbers added together.

a) 

6 + 4 = ...

b) 

8 + 6 = ...

c) 

7 + 7 = ...

3 marks

2 Use the pictures showing how many of each fruit there is to start with to help find the answer to the subtractions.

a) 

12 – 4 = ...

b) 

16 – 9 = ...

c) 

11 – 5 = ...

3 marks

Challenge 2

1 Complete the fact family for each part-whole model.

a) 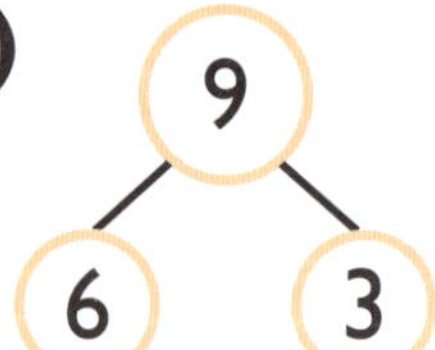

6 + 3 = ...

.... + 6 = 9

9 – 6 = ...

9 – 3 = ...

b) 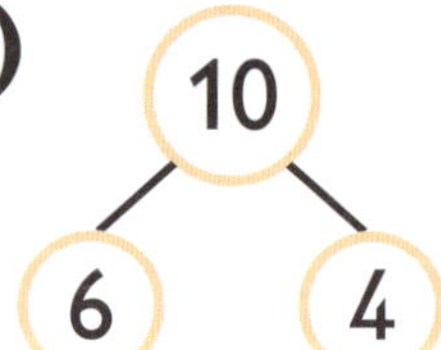

.... + ... = ...

.... + ... = ...

.... – .... = ...

.... – .... = ...

c) 15 → 12, 3

.... + ... = ...
.... + ... = ...
.... – .... = ...
.... – .... = ...

d) 15 → 10, 5

.... + ... = ...
.... + ... = ...
.... – .... = ...
.... – .... = ...

4 marks

2 Complete the number bond pairs.

a) Write the missing number in each number bond pair to 10

7 + ... 2 + ...
5 + ... + 4
.... + 8 1 + ...

b) Write the missing number in each number bond pair to 20

17 + ... 12 + ...
15 + ... + 4
.... + 18 11 + ...

2 marks

Challenge 3

1 Write the missing number in each box to complete the number sentences.

a) 15 + ☐ = 19 **b)** 19 – ☐ = 12

c) ☐ – 2 = 14 **d)** 18 – ☐ = 9

4 marks

2 Write two additions and two subtractions to make each number. The first one has been started for you.

a) (12) 9 + 3 .... 13 – 1 ....

b) (15) ....

c) (8) ....

3 marks

Total: ______ / 19 marks

Had a go ☐ Getting there ☐ Got it! ☐

Counting in multiples of twos, fives and tens

Teaching Note

Counting can be simplified by using multiples of a number. This can also support development of multiplication knowledge.

Challenge 1

1 Count in twos by adding 2 and writing the new number beneath each pair.

a) + + + +

2 4 6 ....

b) + + + +

6 8 .... 12 ....

2 marks

Tip Look for the pattern in the numbers when counting in tens.

2 Count in tens and write in the missing numbers.

a) 10 20 30 .... 50 .... 70 ....

b) .... 40 50 60 .... 80 90 ....

2 marks

Challenge 2

1 Count in fives and write the missing numbers.

5 .... 15 ....

1 mark

2 Count in fives and write the missing numbers on this part of a 100 square.

31	32	33	34	35	36	37	38	39	40
41	42	43	44		46	47	47	49	50
51	52	53	54	55	56	57	58	59	
61	62	63	64	65	66	67	68	69	70
71	72	73	74		76	77	78	79	
81	82	83	84		86	87	88	89	90

1 mark

Tip Use 'jumps' to help with counting on a number line.

Challenge 3

1 Count in twos from each starting number below. The jumps have been added to the first one.

a) 3 + 2 + 2 + 2 + 2 + 2 = ...

(3) 4 5 6 7 8 9 10 11 12 13

b) 37 + 2 + 2 + 2 + 2 + 2 + 2 = ...

37 38 39 40 41 42 43 44 45 46 47 48 49

2 marks

2 Count in fives from the starting number and write the numbers onto the number line.

+5 +5

41 42 43 44 45 ☐ 47 48 49 50 ☐ 52

1 mark

Total: ______ / 9 marks

Had a go ☐ Getting there ☐ Got it! ☐

Grouping and sharing

Teaching Note Grouping and sharing are the first steps in understanding division. Making and recognising groups of equal amounts leads on to exploring division as sharing.

Challenge 1

1 Identify which groups are equal by circling 'True' or 'False'.

a) These two groups are equal. **True** **False**

b) These groups are all equal. **True** **False**

2 marks

2 Add the total number shown in the groups.

a)

5 + 5 + 5 = ...

b)

5 + 5 + 5 + 5 + 5 = ...

2 marks

Teaching Note Explain that the double of a number is that number added to itself such as 1 + 1 = 2, 2 + 2 = 4

Challenge 2

1 Work out the doubles by counting the shapes and writing the amounts in the space provided.

a)

3 + 3 = ...

double 3 is ....

b)

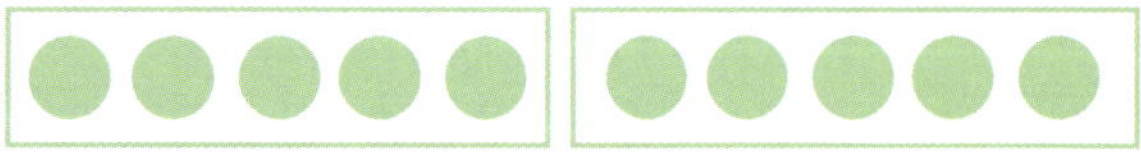

5 + 5 = ...

double 5 is ....

2 marks

Challenge 3

1 Ava has 15 balloons. She shares them equally between herself and four friends. Draw the correct number of balloons next to each child.

1 mark

2 Solve these sharing problems.

a) Ali and his three friends share a pizza equally. There are eight slices.

Each child will get .... slices.

b) Emma has 10 cherries. She says she will share them equally with Carlo and Max.

Explain to an adult what will happen if she tries to do this.

2 marks

Total: ________ / 9 marks

Had a go ☐ Getting there ☐ Got it! ☐

Telling the time

Teaching Note Ensure that there is an understanding that the shorter hand on the clock face indicates the hour. When half past times are shown, the hour hand points halfway between the numbers of the previous and next hour times.

Challenge 1

1 Write the o'clock time for each of the clocks below.

a) 

.... o'clock

b) 

.... o'clock

c) 

.... o'clock

3 marks

2 Draw the hour hand on each clock to show the correct time.

a) 

2 o'clock

b) 

9 o'clock

c) 

5 o'clock

3 marks

3 Draw the hour and minute hand on each clock to show the correct time.

a) 

3 o'clock

b) 

10 o'clock

c) 

6 o'clock

3 marks

Challenge 2

1 On each of these clocks, the minute hand has travelled halfway around the clock. This makes the time half past. Look at the time the hour hand has just moved past to write the times shown on the clocks.

a) 

half past ....

b) 

half past ....

c) 

half past ....

3 marks

2 Draw the minute hand to show the correct time.

a) 

half past 3

b) 

half past 8

c) 

half past 11

3 marks

3 Draw the hour and minute hand to show the correct time.

a) 

half past 1

b) 

half past 6

c) 

half past 9

3 marks

Challenge 3

1 Beth says the time is seven o'clock.
What mistake has Beth made?

....

1 mark

2 Ki says the clock she has drawn shows half past four.
What mistake has Ki made?

....

1 mark

Total: ______ / 20 marks

Had a go ☐ Getting there ☐ Got it! ☐

Progress test 3

1. Draw lines to match each 3-D shape to its name.

a)  b)  c)  d)  e) 

cube **sphere** **cuboid** **pyramid** **cylinder**

5 marks

2. Complete the number bonds to make 20 each time.

a) 11 + ... = 20 b) .... + 7 = 20

c) 15 + ... = 20 d) .... + 8 = 20

e) 3 + ... = 20 f) .... + 10 = 20

6 marks

3. Complete the sentences.

a) 

The rocket is .... cans tall.

b) 

The plane is .... cars long.

2 marks

4. Fill in the missing numbers on the number lines.

a) .... 73 74 .... 76 .... 78 .... 81 82

b) .... 9 .... 6 .... 4 3 2 1 ....

2 marks

5. Use the number lines to find the amount less than the circled starting number. Write the full subtraction sentence each time.

a)

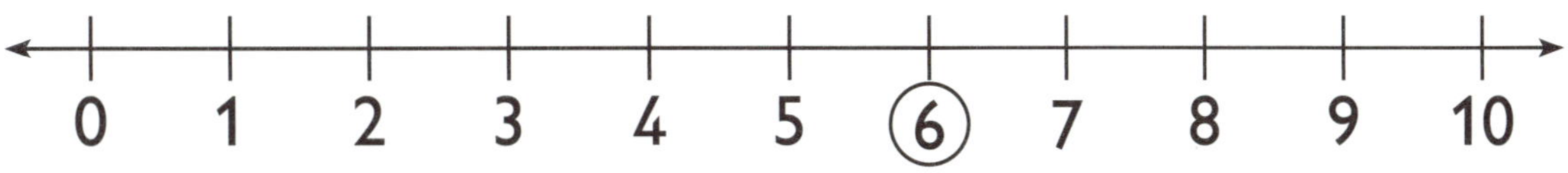

4 less than 6 is .... − .... = ...

b)

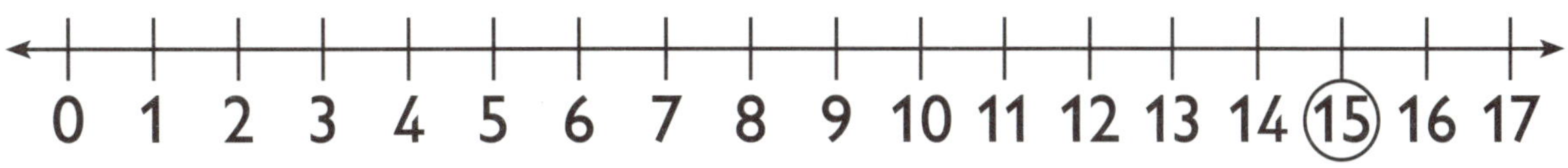

8 less than 15 is .... − .... = ...

2 marks

6. Draw a square around the 2-D shapes and a circle around the 3-D shapes.

1 mark

7. Count the fruit to help find the total of the two numbers added together.

a)

10 + 3 = ...

b)

9 + 7 = ...

2 marks

Progress test 3

8. Count in twos, tens or fives and write in the missing numbers.

a) 0, 10, ___, ___, ___, 50, 60, ___, 80, ___

b) 42, 40, ___, 36, 34, ___, 30, 28, ___, ___, 22, ___

c) ___, ___, 55, 60, 65, ___, ___, 80, ___, 90, 95, 100

3 marks

9. Identify whether the groups in each question are equal by circling 'Equal' or 'Not equal'.

a) **Equal** **Not equal**

b) **Equal** **Not equal**

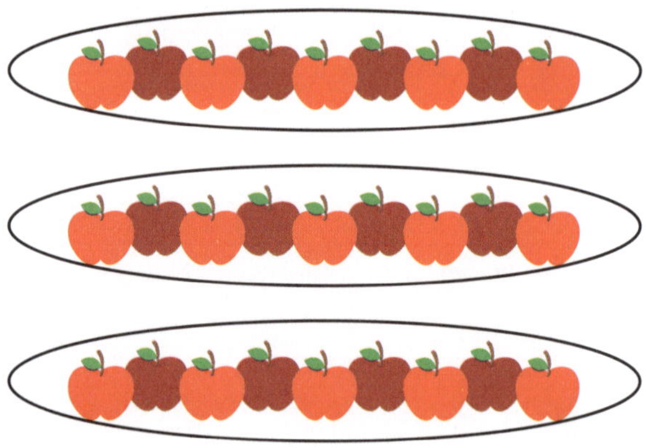

2 marks

10. Draw the hour and minute hand on each clock to show the correct time.

a)

2 o'clock

b)

10 o'clock

c)

7 o'clock

3 marks

11. Use the pictures showing the number of each animal there is to start with to help to find the answer to the subtractions.

a) 

11 – 7 = ...

b) 

17 – 8 = ...

c) 

19 – 9 = ...

d) 

12 – 6 = ...

4 marks

12. Only half of each set of shapes has been drawn. Complete each set by drawing the other half to double the amount and complete the statements.

a) 

6 is half of ....

Double 6 is ....

b) 

9 is half of ....

Double 9 is ....

c) 

7 is half of ....

Double 7 is ....

d) 

8 is half of ....

Double 8 is ....

4 marks

Total: ______ / 36 marks

Audio test 5

The questions for this test are found on the audio available on the QR code above. Listen to each question and write your answers in the spaces below. Try to answer the questions in the time allowed on the audio.

1. **a)** 14 – .... = 4 **b)** .... – 11 = 9

2 marks

2. ☐ ☐

1 mark

3.

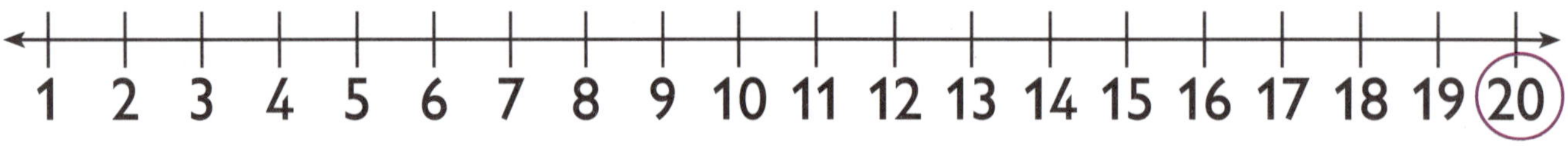

8 less than 20 is ....

1 mark

4.

1 mark

5. ....

1 mark

6.

1 mark

Total: ______ / 7 marks

Had a go ☐ Getting there ☐ Got it! ☐

Audio test 6

Test Questions

The questions for this test are found on the audio available on the QR code above. Listen to each question and write your answers in the spaces below. Try to answer the questions in the time allowed on the audio.

1. **a)**  **b)**  **c)** 

half past 1 **half past 5** **half past 9**

1 mark

2.

109			112		114		

1 mark

3. ....

1 mark

4. 

....

1 mark

5. Double 4 is ....

1 mark

6.  16 – 5 = ...

1 mark

7. **a)** 17 + ... = 20

b) 13 + ... = 20

2 marks

Total: ______ / 8 marks

Had a go ☐ Getting there ☐ Got it! ☐

Addition and subtraction 3

Teaching Note Encourage the use of number lines and part-whole models if automatic recall of number bonds is not yet secure.

Challenge 1

1 Using knowledge of number bonds, complete each addition with the missing number.

a) 12 + ... = 20 **b)** 2 + ... = 20 **c)** 15 + ... = 20

3 marks

2 Using knowledge of number bonds, complete each subtraction with the missing number.

a) 20 – .... = 7 **b)** 10 – .... = 4 **c)** 20 – .... = 5

3 marks

Challenge 2

1 Read and listen to the following sentence. In the space provided, complete the addition problem.

Eve finds six shells. Dev gives her 12 more. How many does she have altogether?

+ =

1 mark

2 Read and listen to the following sentence. In the space provided, complete the subtraction problem.

Max makes 11 sandcastles. The sea washes away four of them. How many are left?

– =

1 mark

Challenge 3

1 Write two subtraction facts for each addition fact. One has been done for you.

9 + 6 = 15
15 – 6 = 9
15 – 9 = 6

a) 13 + 7 = 20

....

....

b) 11 + 8 = 19

....

....

c) 16 + 4 = 20

....

....

3 marks

2 Complete the subtractions below, then write another subtraction fact and two addition facts for each fact family.

a) 17 – 12 = ...

.... – .... = ...

.... + ... = ...

.... + ... = ...

b) 19 – 13 = ...

.... – .... = ...

.... + ... = ...

.... + ... = ...

2 marks

3 Write one addition and one subtraction number sentence to go with this pair of tens frames.

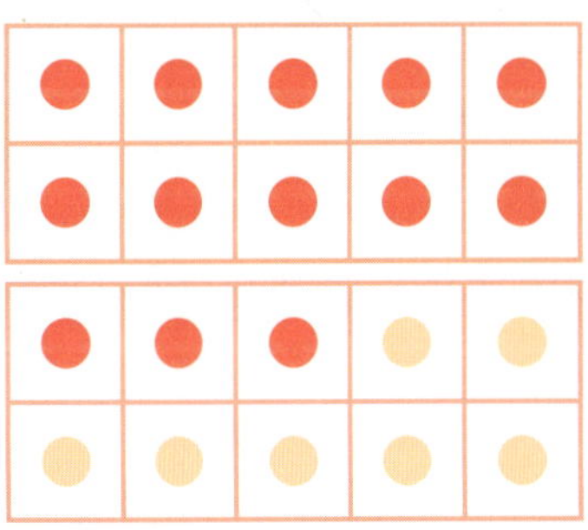

1 mark

4 Explain the mistake below to an adult and then write the correct answer.

Kel says that if 6 + 4 = 10, then 20 = 16 + 14.

What has Kel done wrong? 20 = 16 + ...

1 mark

Total: ______ / 15 marks

Had a go ☐ Getting there ☐ Got it! ☐

Quarter

Teaching Note

Just as dividing a whole shape or amount into two equal parts gives two halves, dividing the whole into four equal parts gives four **quarters**. There are four quarters in a whole.

Challenge 1

1 What fraction of each shape is shaded? Write $\frac{1}{4}$ or $\frac{1}{2}$.

a) 

b) 

c) 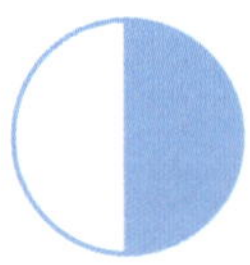

d) 

4 marks

2 Shade one quarter of each shape.

a) 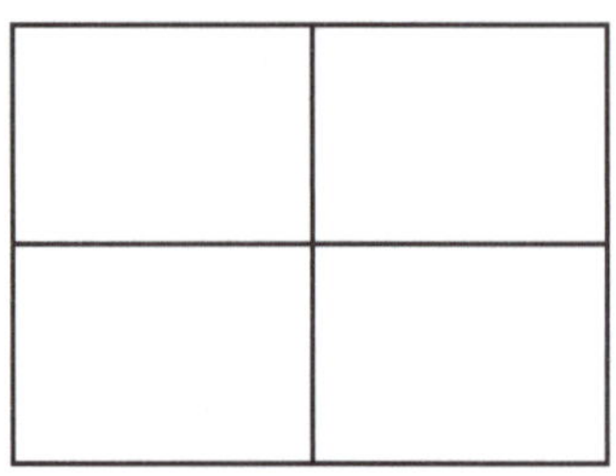

b) 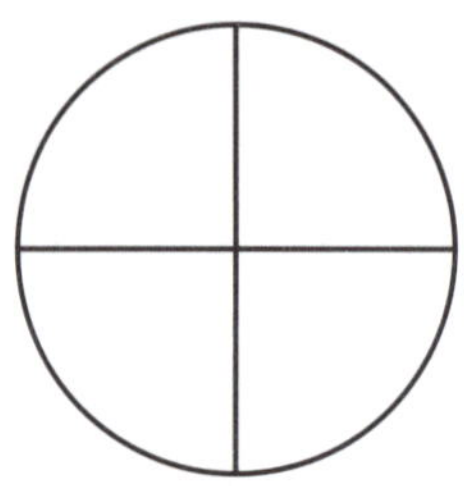

c) 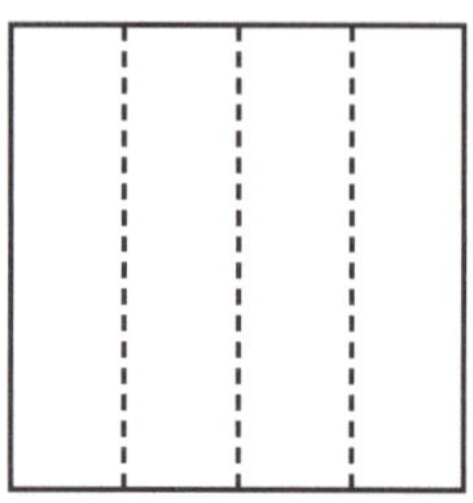

3 marks

Tip

When finding quarters of a quantity, each quarter must be the same amount.

3 Find four different ways of showing quarters on this square. One has been done for you.

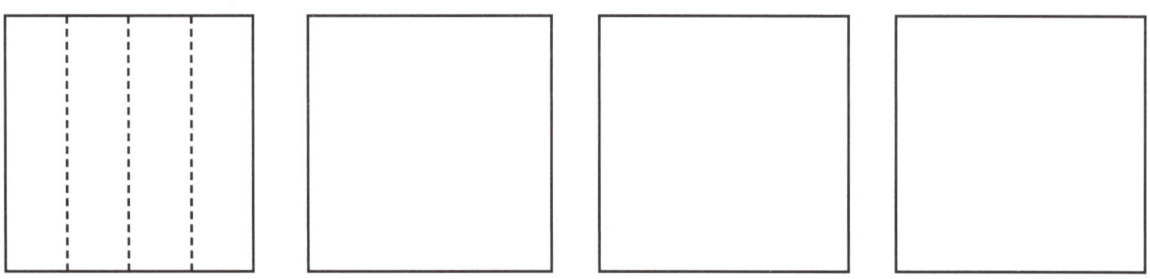

3 marks

Challenge 2

1 Tick (✓) the picture that shows the total number of balls divided into four quarters.

 ☐ 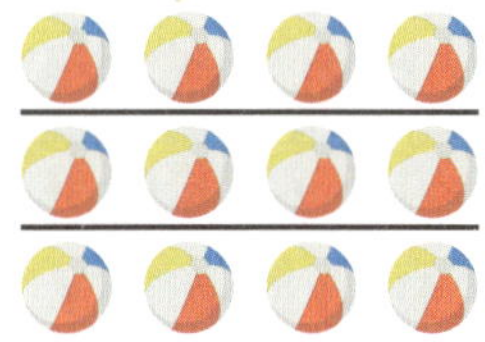 ☐

1 mark

2 Draw lines to split each set of objects into quarters. Complete the sentence to show a quarter of the amount. One has been done for you.

quarter of 8 = 2

a) 

quarter of 12 = ☐

b) 

quarter of 4 = ☐

2 marks

Challenge 3

1 Only a quarter of the following set of shapes has been drawn. Complete the set of shapes by drawing the other quarters and completing the sentence with the full amount.

3 is quarter of ....

1 mark

2 Complete the sentences.

a) 

A quarter of 20 is ....

b) 

A quarter of 16 is ....

2 marks

Total: ______ / 16 marks

Had a go ☐ Getting there ☐ Got it! ☐

Money

Teaching Note

Real coins and notes need to be seen and handled to get an appreciation of what they look and feel like. Where possible, use real coins for sorting activities to help with recognition of the different denominations. Discuss the symbols p for pence and £ for pounds.

Challenge 1

1 Draw lines to match the coins to their correct value.

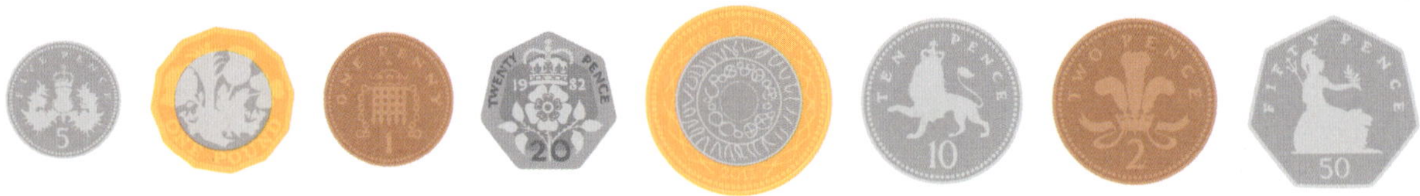

1p | 2p | 5p | 10p | 20p | 50p | £1 | £2

8 marks

2 Complete each part-whole model to show the total value of the coins shown in each part.

a)

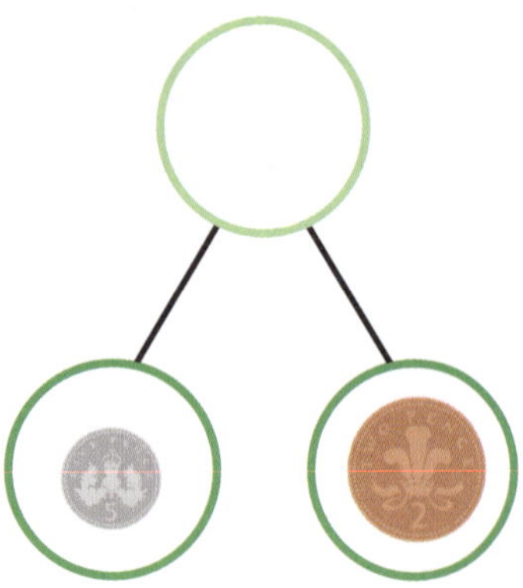

b)

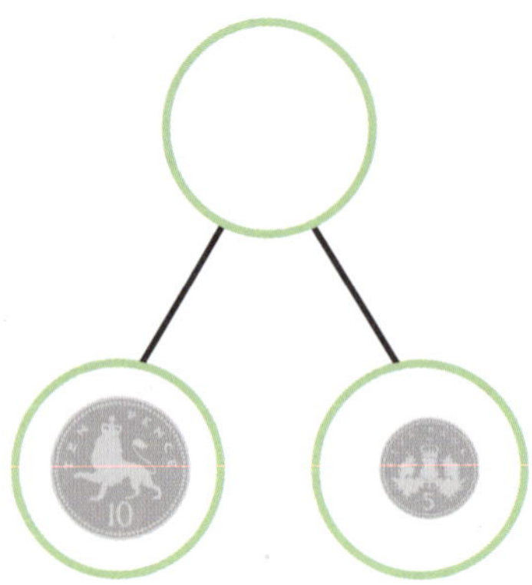

c)

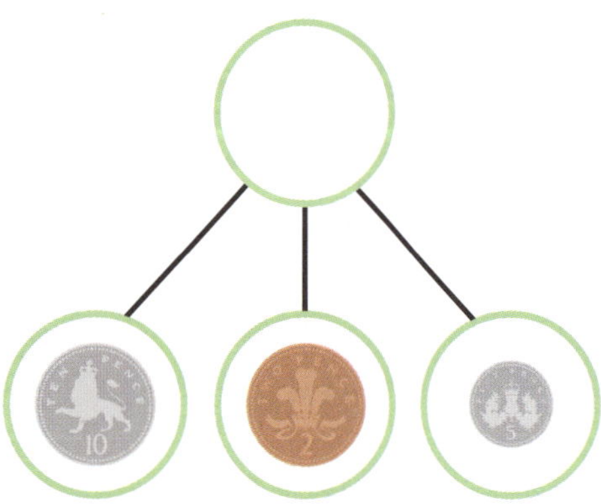

d)

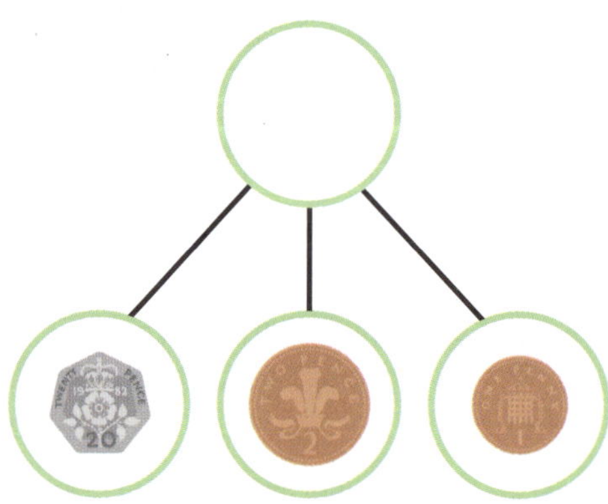

4 marks

Challenge 2

1 Who has more money?

a) **Jack** **Ali**

.... has more money.

b) **Cassy** **Meg**

.... has more money.

2 marks

Challenge 3

1 Write how much money each person has.

a)

Grace has .... p.

b)

Elsa has £........ .

2 marks

2 Show each amount in a different way.

a) Dan has a 5p coin. Draw coins to show two other ways of making 5p. One has been done for you.

b) Izzy has a 20p coin. Draw the coins to show two other ways of making 20p using no more than four coins.

2 marks

Total: ______ / 18 marks

Had a go ☐ Getting there ☐ Got it! ☐

Mass, capacity and volume

Teaching Note Discuss the terms **mass**, **capacity** and **volume** to enable an understanding that mass is how heavy an object is, while capacity and volume allow us to compare how much space is taken or available.

Challenge 1

1 Look at the objects on each set of balancing scales. Complete the sentences with the words **heavier** or **lighter**.

a) 

The train is .... than the apple.

b) 

The teddy is .... than the doll.

2 marks

2 The scales below are balanced. Write how many cubes the mass of each object is equal to.

a) 

The mass of the bottle is .... cubes.

b) 

The mass of the book is .... cubes.

2 marks

Challenge 2

1 Match the labels to describe the volume of water in each beaker. One has been done for you.

a) 

b) 

c) 

d) 

Largest volume	No water	Second largest volume	Smallest volume

3 marks

2 Tick (✓) the box under the container with the greater capacity in each pair of pictures.

a) 

b) 

c) 

3 marks

Challenge 3

1 Who has the heaviest and lightest pets?

a) Jack's kitten has a mass the same as 28 cubes.

Raja's cat has a mass the same as 43 cubes.

The heaviest pet belongs to ....

b) Lena's rabbit has a mass the same as 39 cubes.

Stan's puppy has a mass the same as 63 cubes.

The lightest pet belongs to ....

2 marks

2 Anna has this much juice in her water bottle.

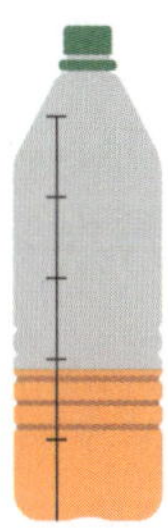

Sabina has this much.

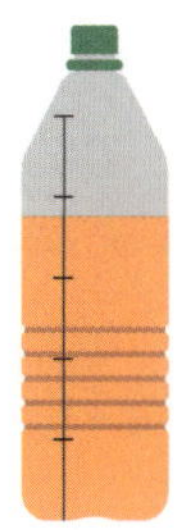

.... has the greatest volume of juice.

1 mark

3 Elan half fills her shopping bag with four cakes.

Stef fills his bag completely full with seven cakes.

.... has the bag with the largest capacity.

1 mark

Total: ______ / 14 marks

Had a go ☐ Getting there ☐ Got it! ☐

Position and direction

Teaching Note As well as being given the opportunity to investigate different sizes and directions of turn with real objects, children will need to revisit the terms (and meanings) half and quarter for turns before being shown three-quarter turns.

Challenge 1

1 Complete the statements about the shapes shown below using the words **left** or **right**.

a) The triangle is the shape to the .... of the square.

b) The square is two places to the .... of the circle.

c) The circle is three places to the .... of the rectangle.

3 marks

2 Recognise turns.

Each arrow below has turned to the **right**. Match each arrow with the correct picture of a pencil that has also made turns to the right. The first one has been done for you.

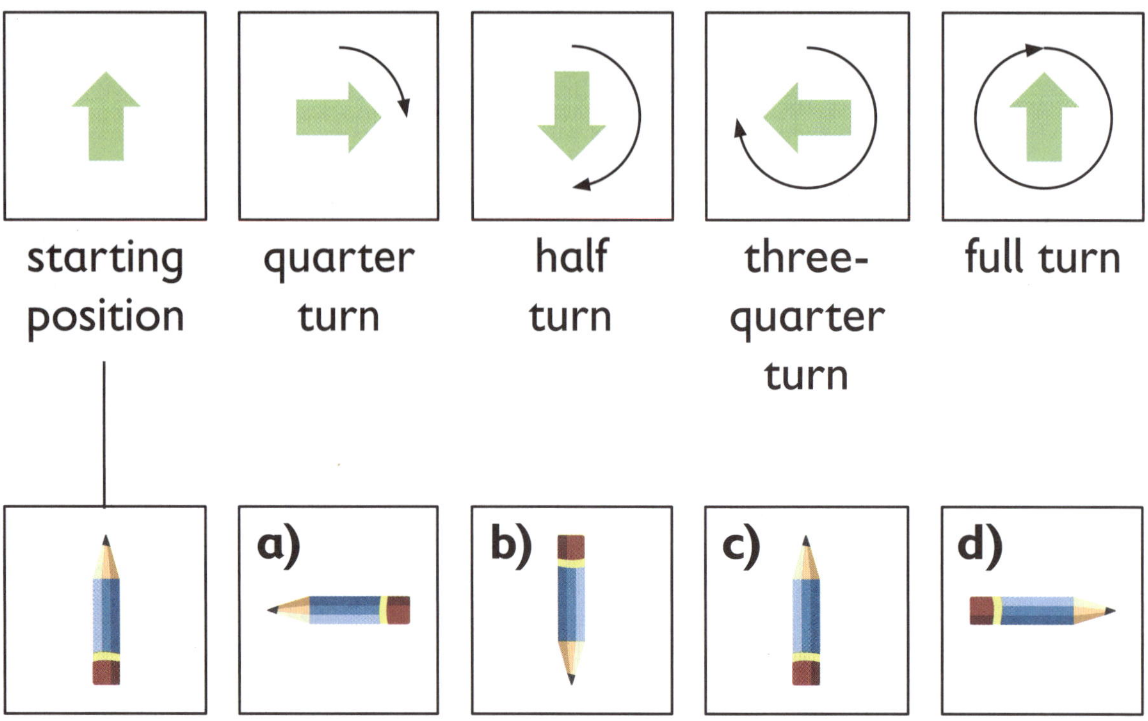

4 marks

Challenge 2

1 Look at the picture. Tick (✓) the statements below that correctly describe the position of the objects.

a) The teddy is on top of the box. ☐

b) The teddy is between the plane and the car. ☐

c) The teddy is next to the book. ☐

d) The teddy is in front of the box. ☐

e) The teddy is between the train and the car. ☐

☐ 2 marks

Challenge 3

1 Follow the directions and draw each triangle in its new position.

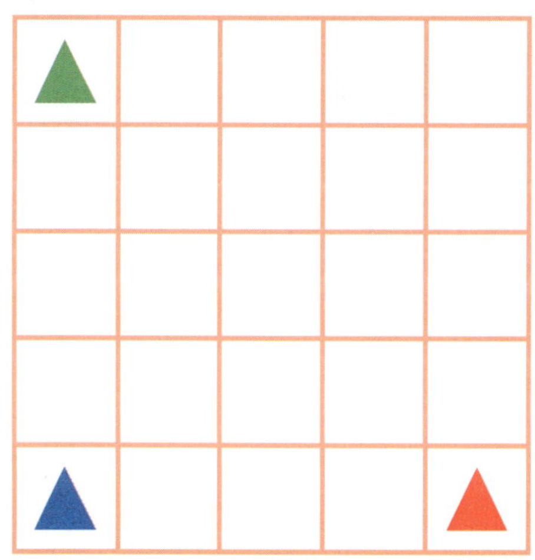

a) The red triangle moves up three spaces, left two spaces and down one space.

b) The green triangle moves down two spaces, right two spaces and up two spaces.

c) The blue triangle moves up one space, right one space, up two spaces and right three spaces.

☐ 3 marks

Total: ______ / 12 marks

Had a go ☐ Getting there ☐ Got it! ☐

Progress test 4

1. Complete each number sentence by writing the missing number in each box.

a) 11 + ☐ = 18 **b)** 17 – ☐ = 13

c) 19 – ☐ = 4 **d)** ☐ – 2 = 18

e) 16 + ☐ = 19 **f)** ☐ – 12 = 3

6 marks

2. Lucy has 18 sweets.

a) She shares her sweets equally with Jack. Draw the correct number of sweets next to each person.

b) Lucy and Jack are joined by another friend. How many sweets will each child have if they are shared equally? Draw the sweets in three groups below to help you.

They will have .... sweets each.

2 marks

3. Emma has 10 raspberries. She shares them equally with Carlo.

How many raspberries will each child have? ....

1 mark

4. **Draw the hour and minute hand on each clock to show the correct time.**

a) 

half past 12

b) 

half past 2

2 marks

5. **Look at the information below. In the space provided, complete each addition or subtraction problem.**

a) The squirrel has 8 acorns. It collects 11 more. How many acorns does it have altogether?

+ =

b) Jen collects 13 leaves. Esme collects 7 more. How many do they have altogether?

+ =

c) Kyle has 17 conkers. He gives 12 of them to his friends. How many conkers does he then have?

– =

3 marks

Progress test 4

6. Write two addition and two subtraction number sentences to go with each pair of tens frames.

a)

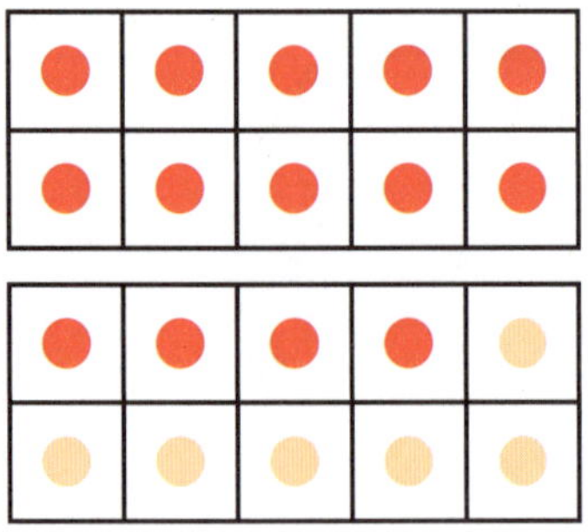

..... + ... = ...

..... + ... = ...

..... – ..... = ...

..... – ..... = ...

b)

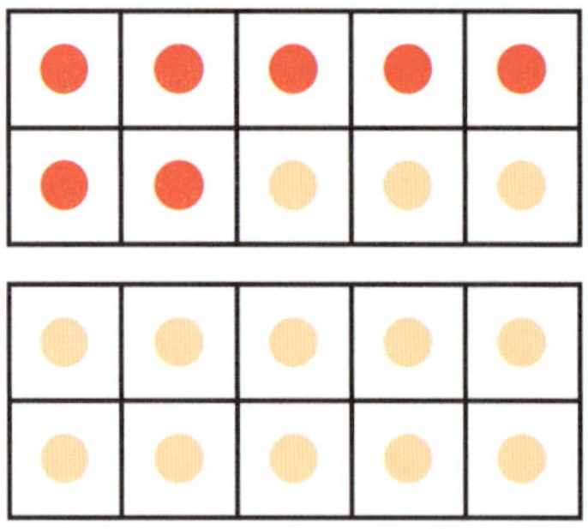

..... + ... = ...

..... + ... = ...

..... – ..... = ...

..... – ..... = ...

2 marks

7. Shade the shapes as instructed.

a) Shade a quarter of each shape below.

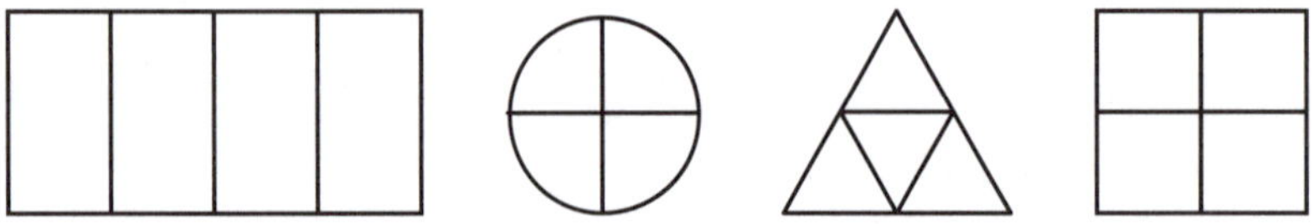

b) Shade half of each shape below.

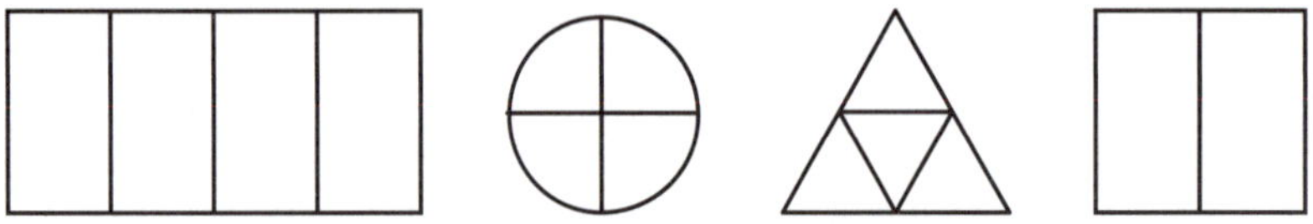

8 marks

8. Who has more money?

a)

Sam

Elsa

.... has more money.

b) 

Mo Jess

.... has more money.

2 marks

9. Draw a line to match each arrow to the description of how much it has turned from the starting position.

start	three-quarter turn to right	half turn	quarter turn to right	full turn

4 marks

10. Complete each part-whole model to show the total value of the coins shown in each part.

a) 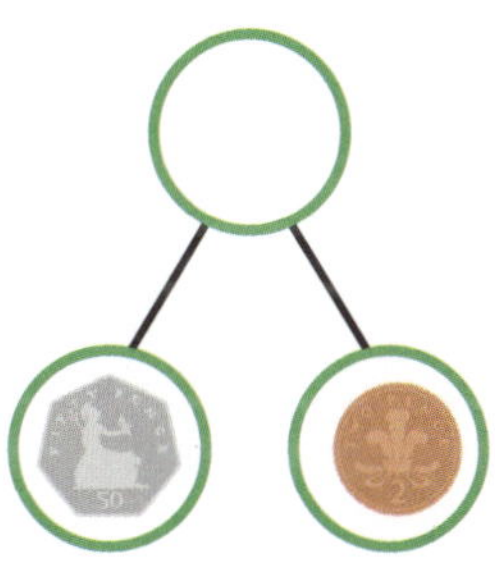

b) 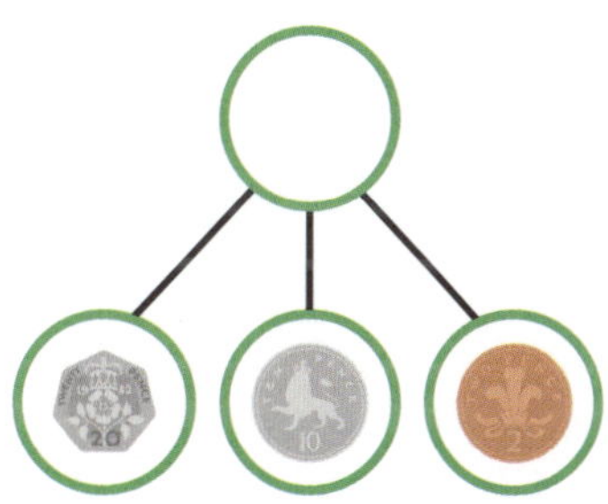

c) 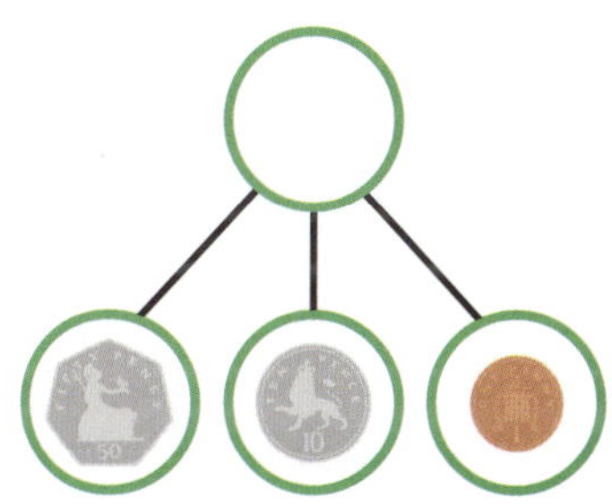

3 marks

11. Write the missing numbers in each sequence.

a) 17 15 13 .... 9 .... 3 ....

b) .... 18 23 28 .... 43 48 ....

2 marks

Total: ______ / 35 marks

Audio test 7

The questions for this test are found on the audio available on the QR code above. Listen to each question and write your answers in the spaces below. Try to answer the questions in the time allowed on the audio.

1. **a)** 20 – .... = 14 **b)** 10 – .... = 2

2 marks

2. ....

1 mark

3. **Jack**

Ali

1 mark

4.

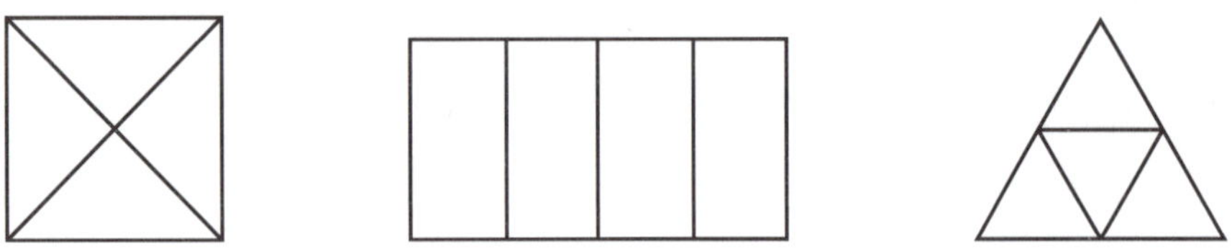

3 marks

5.

.... p

1 mark

6.

1 mark

7.

2 marks

Total: ________ **/ 11 marks**

Had a go ☐ Getting there ☐ Got it! ☐

Audio test 8

Test Questions

The questions for this test are found on the audio available on the QR code above. Listen to each question and write your answers in the spaces below. Try to answer the questions in the time allowed on the audio.

1. 

203 .... 199 .... 196 195 194

1 mark

2.  ....

1 mark

3. 

....

1 mark

4.  

1 mark

5. 

£ ....

1 mark

6. Josie has .... red fish. 

Josie has .... blue fish. 

2 marks

Total: ______ / 7 marks

Had a go ☐ Getting there ☐ Got it! ☐

Answers

Pages 6–9

1. Numbers read correctly and clearly written in the correct order **[2]**
2. **a)** 3, 5, 7, 8, 10
   b) Counters added for 2, 5, 6, 8 and 9 **[2]**
3. **a)** 5, 6, 7 **b)** 8, 9, 10 **[2]**
4. **a)** 2 **b)** 4 **c)** 3 **d)** 5 **[4]**
5. **a)** 3 **b)** 4 **c)** 4 **d)** 5 **[4]**
6. **a)** 2 **b)** 3 **c)** 4 **d)** 3 **[4]**
7. **a)** yellow flowers ticked **b)** blue flowers ticked **[2]**
8. **a)** More than 7 circles drawn
   b) More than 5 squares drawn **[2]**
9. **a)** Less than 5 circles drawn
   b) Less than 8 squares drawn **[2]**
10. **a)** 2 more circles **b)** 5 more squares
    c) 4 more circles **d)** 6 more squares **[4]**
11. **a)** 10 **b)** 10 **c)** 10 **d)** 10 **[4]**

Pages 10–11

Challenge 1

1. **a)** 7 **b)** 6 **c)** 11 **d)** 15 **e)** 6 **f)** 9 **[6]**

Challenge 2

1. **a)** 17 = seventeen; 12 = twelve; 3 = three; 9 = nine; 20 = twenty **[5]**
2. **a)** Fifteen **[1]**

Challenge 3

1. **a)** 4, 5, 9 **b)** 8, 12, 15 **c)** 14, 16, 19 **[3]**
2. **a)** ten, thirteen **b)** eighteen, sixteen **[2]**

Pages 12–13

Challenge 1

1. Check one more shape has been drawn. New totals:
   a) 5 **b)** 3 **c)** 10 **d)** 17 **[4]**

Challenge 2

1. **a)** 13 **b)** 10 **c)** 14 **d)** 6 **[4]**

Challenge 3

1. **a)** 8 **b)** 18 **c)** 3 **d)** 13
   e) 8 **f)** 10 **g)** 9 **h)** 19 **[8]**
2. **a)** more **b)** less **c)** less **d)** less
   e) more **f)** less **[6]**

Pages 14–15

Challenge 1

1. **a)** most, least **b)** least, most **[2]**

Challenge 2

1. **a)** 9 rectangles drawn **b)** 13 circles drawn **[2]**
2. **a)** 2 additional squares drawn
   b) 13 additional triangles drawn **[2]**

Challenge 3

1. **a)** less than **b)** equal to **c)** more than
   d) equal to **e)** more than **f)** less than **[6]**
2. **a)** must be 5 is equal to 5; **b)** to **e)** multiple options – check all are correct **[5]**

Pages 16–17

Challenge 1

1. **a)** parts 3 and 3, whole 6 **b)** parts 5 and 4, whole 9 **c)** parts 6 and 3, whole 9 **[3]**
2. **a)** whole 5; 3, 2 or 1, 4 or 5, 0
   b) whole 8; 1, 7 or 6, 2 or 5, 3 or 4, 4 or 8, 0
   c) whole 9; 5, 4 or 0, 9 or 1, 8 or 7, 2 or 6, 3 **[3]**

Challenge 2

1. **a)** 7 **b)** 6 + 2 = 8 **[2]**
2. **a)** 4 + 6 = 10 **b)** 7 + 3 = 10 **[2]**

Challenge 3

1. **a)** 7 + 3 = 10, 3 + 7 = 10
   b) 9 + 1 = 10, 1 + 9 = 10 **[2]**

Pages 18–19

Challenge 1

1. **a)** longer **b)** shorter
   c) shorter **d)** longer **[4]**
2. **a)** taller **b)** shorter **[2]**

Challenge 2

1. **a)** taller person drawn **b)** shorter person drawn **[2]**

Challenge 3

1. **a)** 6 **b)** 1 **[2]**
2. **a)** 6 cm **b)** 12 cm **c)** 7 cm **d)** 9 cm **[4]**

Pages 20–21

Challenge 1

1. Days written in order **[6]**
2. **a)** before **b)** after **c)** after **d)** before **[4]**
3. January, April, June, August, October, November **[6]**
4. **a)** January **b)** December **c)** March **[3]**

Challenge 2

1. **a)** 14 **b)** 21 **[2]**

Challenge 3

1. **a)** 4 **b)** 3
   c) Two full weeks (14 days) highlighted **[3]**

Pages 22–25

1. **a)** 5/five, 8/eight, 11/eleven
   b) thirteen/13, fifteen/15 **[2]**
2. One more of each shape drawn and correct new total given
   a) 8 **b)** 6 **c)** 12 **d)** 15 **[4]**
3. **a)** 9 **b)** 11 **c)** 12 **[3]**
4. **a)** 12 cm **b)** 8 cm **[2]**
5. January, May, August, October **[1]**
6. Longer and shorter lines drawn **[2]**
7. **a)** 7 + 3 = 10, 3 + 7 = 10
   b) 4 + 6 = 10, 6 + 4 = 10
   c) 8 + 2 = 10, 2 + 8 = 10 **[3]**
8. Days in correct order (starting point does not matter) **[1]**
9. **a)** equal to **b)** less than **c)** more than **[3]**
10. **a)** 14 and 16 **b)** 16 **[2]**
11. He has not put the 8 (the total amount) as the whole. **[1]**
12. A representation of a flower taller than and a flower shorter than the girl **[2]**

Page 26

1. Seven, eight (or 7, 8) **[1]**
2. First line ticked **[1]**
3. Friday **[1]**
4. October **[1]**
5. 9 **[1]**
6. 10, 11 and 17 circled **[1]**
7. 10 **[1]**
8. 8 + 2 = 10 **[1]**

Page 27

1. Four more counters drawn. **[1]**
2. 13 **[1]**
3. Monday **[1]**
4. 6 and 1 or 5 and 2 or 4 and 3 or 7 and 0 **[1]**
5. Third snake ticked **[1]**
6. 14 **[1]**
7. Five and twelve circled **[1]**
8. 5 + 3 = 8 **[1]**

Pages 28–29

Challenge 1

1. 9, 12, 16, 23, 32, 45, 54, 61, 70, 78, 87, 89, 93, 94, 100 **[15]**

Challenge 2

1. **a)** 33, 34, 36, 39, 41 **b)** 68, 70, 72, 73, 75 **[2]**
2. **a)** 52, 51, 49, 46, 45 **b)** 100, 97, 96, 94, 91 **[2]**

Challenge 3

1. **a)** 45, 47, 55, 56, 64, 66, 74, 77
   b) 68, 69, 77, 78, 79, 80, 87, 98 **[2]**
2. **a)** 98, 100, 101, 103, 106 **b)** 103, 101, 100, 99 **[2]**
3. 136, 137, 138, 139, 140, 141 **[1]**
4. 202, 201, 200, 199, 198, 197 **[1]**

Pages 30–31

Challenge 1

1. **a)** part-whole model 8, 4, 4, answer = 8
   b) part-whole model 9, 6, 3, answer = 9 **[2]**

Challenge 2

1. **a)** 5 – 1 = 4 **b)** 10 – 1 = 9 **[2]**

Challenge 3

1. **a)** 4 more than 5 is 9, 5 + 4 = 9
   b) 7 more than 8 is 15, 8 + 7 = 15 **[2]**
2. **a)** 9 less than 9 is 0, 9 – 9 = 0
   b) 5 less than 17 is 12, 17 – 5 = 12 **[2]**

Pages 32–33

Challenge 1

1. **a)** 6 **b)** 8 **[2]**

Challenge 2

1. **a)** 5 groups of two; 2 + 2 + 2 + 2 + 2 = 10
   b) 4 groups of five; 5 + 5 + 5 + 5 = 20 **[2]**

Challenge 3

1. **a)** 6 **b)** 12 **[2]**
2. **a)** 7 by 2 array drawn = 14
   b) 3 by 3 array drawn = 9 **[2]**

Pages 34–35

Challenge 1

1. **a)** before **b)** after **[2]**
2. **a)** later **b)** earlier **[2]**
3. Check sentences are correct **[2]**

Challenge 2

1. **a)** False, True, True **b)** 8 o'clock
   c) 12 o'clock **[5]**

Challenge 3

1. **a)** True, True, False **b)** Neesa **c)** Molly **[5]**

Pages 36–37

Challenge 1

1. Half of each shape shaded **[3]**
2. Second and third shapes ticked **[2]**

Challenge 2

1. Each shape divided into two equal parts **[4]**
2. $\frac{1}{2}$ written under first and third pizzas **[2]**

Challenge 3

1. **a)** Art split into two 4s, Half of 8 = 4
   b) Art split into two 2s, Half of 4 = 2 **[2]**
2. **a)** 5 more circles drawn, 5 is half of 10
   b) 6 more triangles drawn, 6 is half of 12
   c) 2 more squares drawn, 2 is half of 4
   d) 8 more circles drawn, 8 is half of 16 **[4]**

Pages 38–39

Challenge 1

1. **a)** square **b)** rectangle **c)** circle **d)** triangle **[4]**
2. **a)** 4 **b)** 3 **c)** 4 **d)** triangle **[4]**

Challenge 2

1. **a)** cube **b)** pyramid **c)** sphere
   d) cuboid **e)** cylinder **[5]**

Challenge 3

1. **a)** 3 triangles circled **b)** 3 squares circled
   c) 3 cuboids circled **[3]**
2. **a)** 1 triangle and 2 squares circled
   b) 1 cylinder, 1 cuboid and 1 pyramid circled **[2]**

Pages 40–43

1. **a)** She is wrong. Her stick person is 9 cm tall.
   b) False **[2]**
2. **a)** 12, 14, 21, 23, 33, 34, 41, 42
   b) 57, 58, 66, 69, 76, 77, 87, 88, 89 **[2]**
3. 1, 2, 4, 3, 5 **[1]**
4. **a)** 6 groups, 3 + 3 + 3 + 3 + 3 + 3 = 18
   b) 4 groups, 4 + 4 + 4 + 4 = 16 **[2]**
5. **a)** and **d)** circled **[2]**
6. **a)** 11 and 9 **b)** 18 and 16 **[2]**
7. **a)** 4 **b)** 5 **c)** 6 **[3]**
8. 4 whole pizzas **[1]**
9. **a)** triangle **b)** square **c)** circle **[3]**
10. Drawing of 5 and 4 or 4 and 4 with 1 left over to show that there cannot be two equal groups **[1]**
11. **a)** 9 **b)** 3 **c)** 6 **d)** 2
    e) 5 **f)** 10 **[6]**
12. **a)** 2 **b)** 14 **c)** 7 **[3]**

Page 44

1. Line drawn horizontally, vertically or diagonally through the centre of the rectangle **[1]**
2. 15, 16 **[1]**
3. Shorter line drawn **[1]**
4. 10 **[1]**
5. 13 **[1]**
6. 2 **[1]**
7. 5 **[1]**

Page 45

1. First and fourth shapes ticked **[1]**
2. 8 **[1]**
3. 32, 31, 30, 28, 27 **[1]**
4. 10 **[1]**
5. 3 **[1]**
6. **a)** one o'clock **b)** three o'clock **[2]**

Pages 46–47

Challenge 1

1. **a)** 10 **b)** 14 **c)** 14 **[3]**
2. **a)** 8 **b)** 7 **c)** 6 **[3]**

Challenge 2

1. **a)** 6 + 3 = 9, 3 + 6 = 9, 9 – 6 = 3, 9 – 3 = 6
   b) 6 + 4 = 10, 4 + 6 = 10, 10 – 6 = 4, 10 – 4 = 6
   c) 12 + 3 = 15, 3 + 12 = 15, 15 – 12 = 3, 15 – 3 = 12
   d) 10 + 5 = 15, 5 + 10 = 15, 15 – 10 = 5, 15 – 5 = 10 **[4]**
2. **a)** 3, 8, 5, 6, 2, 9 **b)** 3, 8, 5, 16, 2, 9 **[2]**

Challenge 3

1. **a)** 4 **b)** 7 **c)** 16 **d)** 9 **[4]**
2. Answers will vary. Ensure there are two correct additions and subtractions for each number **[3]**

Pages 48–49

Challenge 1

1. **a)** 8, 10 **b)** 10, 14 **[2]**
2. **a)** 40, 60, 80 **b)** 30, 70, 100 **[2]**

Challenge 2

1. 10, 20, 25 **[1]** 2. 45, 60, 75, 80, 85 **[1]**

Challenge 3

1. **a)** 13 **b)** 49 **[2]**
2. 46, 51 **[1]**

Pages 50–51

Challenge 1

1. **a)** True **b)** False [2]
2. **a)** 15 **b)** 25 [2]

Challenge 2

1. **a)** 6 **b)** 10 [2]

Challenge 3

1. 3 balloons next to each child [1]
2. **a)** 2 **b)** An explanation that acknowledges that they will get three each but there will be one remaining. [2]

Pages 52–53

Challenge 1

1. **a)** 4 **b)** 7 **c)** 1 [3]
2. Check hour hand is shorter than minute hand.
   a) pointing to 2 **b)** pointing to 9
   c) pointing to 5 [3]
3. Hour and minute hands drawn accurately to show 3, 10 and 6 o'clock [3]

Challenge 2

1. **a)** 2 **b)** 4 **c)** 1 [3]
2. Minute hand pointing to 6 on each clock face [3]
3. Hour and minute hands drawn accurately to show the times; ensure hour hand is between the previous hour and the next hour [3]

Challenge 3

1. Explanation should show an understanding that Beth has got the hour and minute hands the wrong way round. [1]
2. Explanation should show an understanding that Ki needed to make sure the hour hand was halfway between 4 and 5 [1]

Pages 54–57

1. **a)** sphere **b)** cube **c)** cylinder
   d) cuboid **e)** pyramid [5]
2. **a)** 9 **b)** 13 **c)** 5 **d)** 12
   e) 17 **f)** 10 [6]
3. **a)** 5 **b)** 6 [2]
4. **a)** 72, 75, 77, 79, 80 **b)** 10, 8, 7, 5, 0 [2]
5. **a)** 2, 6 – 4 = 2 **b)** 7, 15 – 8 = 7 [2]
6.

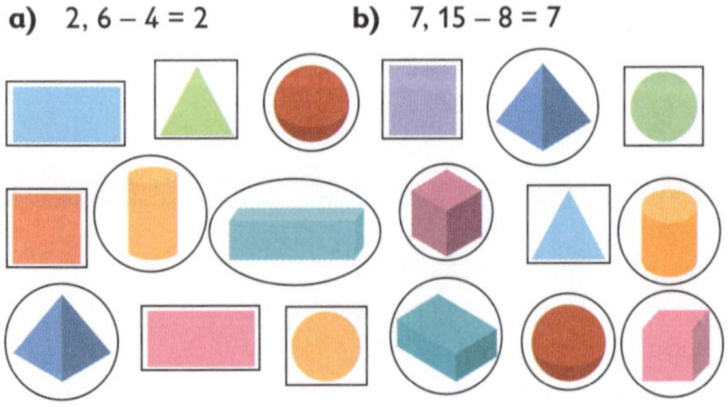

[1]

7. **a)** 13 **b)** 16 [2]
8. **a)** 20, 30, 40, 70, 90 **b)** 38, 32, 26, 24, 20
   c) 45, 50, 70, 75, 85 [3]
9. **a)** Not equal **b)** Equal [2]
10. Hour and minute hands drawn accurately to show 2, 10 and 7 o'clock [3]
11. **a)** 4 **b)** 9 **c)** 10 **d)** 6 [4]
12. **a)** 6 circles drawn, 12 **b)** 9 squares drawn, 18
    c) 7 triangles drawn, 14 **d)** 8 circles drawn, 16 [4]

Page 58

1. **a)** 14 – 10 = 4 **b)** 20 – 11 = 9 [2]
2. Each square divided differently into two equal halves [1]
3. 12 **[1]** **4.** Hands drawn to show 8 o'clock [1]
5. 40, 50, 60 **[1]** **6.** 5 butterflies circled [1]

Page 59

1. **a)** half past 9 **b)** half past 1 **c)** half past 5 [1]
2. 110, 111, 113, 115. 116 [1]
3. 40, 45, 50 **[1]** **4.** 8 [1]
5. 8 **[1]** **6.** 11 [1]
7. **a)** 17 + 3 **b)** 13 + 7 [2]

Pages 60–61

Challenge 1

1. **a)** 8 **b)** 18 **c)** 5 [3]
2. **a)** 13 **b)** 6 **c)** 15 [3]

Challenge 2

1. 6 + 12 = 18 or 12 + 6 = 18 [1]
2. 11 – 4 = 7 [1]

Challenge 3

1. **a)** 20 – 7 = 13, 20 – 13 = 7
   b) 19 – 8 = 11, 19 – 11 = 8
   c) 20 – 4 = 16, 20 – 16 = 4 [3]
2. **a)** 17 – 12 = 5, 17 – 5 = 12, 12 + 5 = 17, 5 + 12 = 17
   b) 19 – 13 = 6, 19 – 6 = 13, 13 + 6 = 19, 6 + 13 = 19 [2]
3. 13 + 7 = 20 or 7 + 13 = 20; 20 – 7 = 13 or 20 – 13 = 7 [1]
4. 20 = 16 + 4 Explanation should recognise that Kel has mistakenly added 10 to both 6 and 4. [1]

Pages 62–63

Challenge 1

1. **a)** $\frac{1}{4}$ **b)** $\frac{1}{2}$ **c)** $\frac{1}{2}$ **d)** $\frac{1}{4}$ [4]
2. One part (quarter) of each shape shaded [3]
3. Ensure each shape has been divided equally into 4 quarters, each in a different way [3]

Challenge 2

1. Tick next to first image [1]
2. Ensure both sets are split into 4 equal amounts.
   a) 3 **b)** 1 [2]

Challenge 3

1. 9 more triangles drawn, 12 [1]
2. **a)** 5 **b)** 4 [2]

Pages 64–65

Challenge 1

1. Lines drawn to correct coins – from left to right: 5p, £1, 1p, 20p, £2, 10p, 2p, 50p [8]
2. **a)** 7p **b)** 15p
   c) 17p **d)** 23p [4]

Challenge 2

1. **a)** Ali **b)** Cassy [2]

Challenge 3

1. **b)** 57p **b)** £17 [2]
2. Coins must add to the total given.
   a) 2p, 2p, 1p or 2p, 1p, 1p, 1p
   b) 2 × 10p; 10p, 5p, 5p; 4 × 5p [2]

Pages 66–67

Challenge 1

1. **a)** heavier **b)** lighter [2]
2. **a)** 6 **b)** 8 [2]

Challenge 2

1. **a)** second largest volume **b)** largest volume
   c) smallest volume [3]
2. **a)** first box ticked **b)** first box ticked
   c) first box ticked [3]

Challenge 3

1. **a)** Raja **b)** Lena [2]
2. Sabina [1]
3. Elan [1]

Pages 68–69

Challenge 1

1. **a)** left **b)** right **c)** left [3]
2. **a)** $\frac{3}{4}$ turn **b)** $\frac{1}{2}$ turn **c)** full turn
   d) $\frac{1}{4}$ turn [4]

Challenge 2

1. **d)** and **e)** ticked [2]

Challenge 3

1.

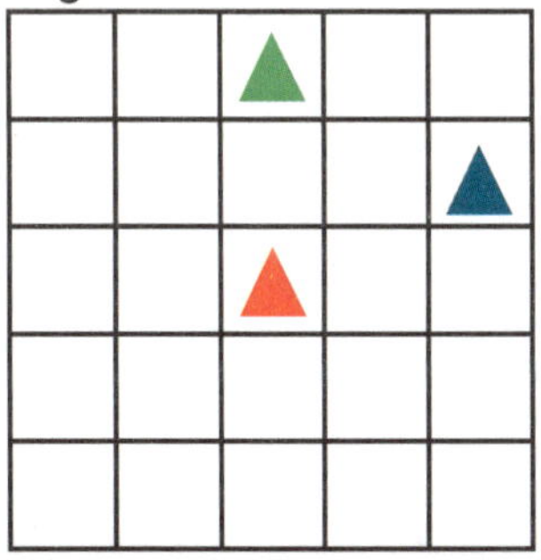

[3]

Pages 70–73

1. **a)** 7 **b)** 4 **c)** 15 **d)** 20
   e) 3 **f)** 15 [6]
2. **a)** 9 sweets drawn for each child **b)** 6 [2]
3. 5 [1]
4. Each time correctly shown with the hour hand between the previous and next hour [2]
5. **a)** 8 + 11 = 19 **b)** 13 + 7 = 20 **c)** 17 – 12 = 5 [3]
6. **a)** 14 + 6 = 20, 6 + 14 = 20, 20 – 14 = 6, 20 – 6 = 14
   b) 7 + 13 = 20, 13 + 7 = 20, 20 – 13 = 7, 20 – 7 = 13 [2]
7. **a)** one quarter of each shape shaded
   b) half (two quarters) of each shape shaded [8]
8. **a)** Elsa **b)** Jess [2]
9. **a)** $\frac{1}{2}$ turn **b)** full turn
   c) $\frac{3}{4}$ turn right **d)** $\frac{1}{4}$ turn right [4]
10. **a)** 52p **b)** 32p **c)** 61p [3]
11. **a)** 11, 7, 5, 1 **b)** 13, 33, 38, 53 [2]

Page 74

1. **a)** 6 **b)** 8 [2]
2. 0 [1]
3. Ali circled [1]
4. One section of each shape shaded [3]
5. 45p [1]
6. Half past four correctly shown with the hour hand between 4 and 5 [1]
7. First beaker to show less than the second. Third beaker to show more than the second. [2]

Page 75

1. 202, 201, 200, 198, 197 [1]
2. 5 [1]
3. half past 10 (or 10:30) [1]
4. Robot circled [1]
5. £12 [1]
6. 6 red fish; 3 blue fish [2]

Fill in your score for each progress test in the window of the rocket.